The HAWAI'I COFFEE Book

The HAWAI'I COFFEE *Book*

A GOURMET'S GUIDE
FROM KONA TO KAUA'I

SHAWN STEIMAN, Ph.D.

WATERMARK
PUBLISHING

ISBN 978-1-948011-16-7

Library of Congress Control Number: 2019905173

Design by Mae Ariola
Production by Dawn Sakamoto Paiva

Watermark Publishing
1000 Bishop St., Suite 806
Honolulu, Hawai'i 96813
Telephone 1-808-587-7766
Toll-free 1-866-900-BOOK
sales@bookshawaii.net
www.bookshawaii.net

Printed in Korea

CONTENTS

No joke

brown
little bean
i laughed because
sensing is like blessing:
simple sensation inspires,
    lifts, bestows

—Julia Wieting

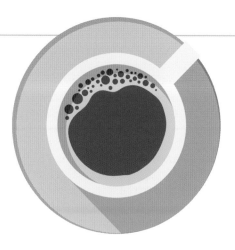

INTRODUCTION

IN THE 11 YEARS since this book was first published, the Hawai'i coffee industry has evolved and matured. The number of coffee farms has steadily increased such that there are now more coffee farms than there has been for decades; specialty coffee cafés serving bespoke brews are the norm; the industry survived a crisis brought on by the arrival of the coffee berry borer; and farms and cafés are pursuing novel, often technology-rich, tools to create ever more diverse and compelling coffees.

This new edition offers a fresh look at the industry. The old material has been revisited and, if necessary, updated. New material has been added to capture the evolution and development that has occurred locally and sometimes internationally. New recipes—collected from Hawai'i chefs, bartenders, bakers and food makers—offer a multitude of ways to include coffee in your glass and on your plate. The pace of change is so rapid in the industry now, that rather than a printed directory of farms, tours and cafés, as appeared in the original edition, an online resource guide will be posted at www.coffeaconsulting.com.

While Hawai'i is still known worldwide for its specialty 100 percent Kona coffee, true coffee lovers know that Kona is only part of the story. In the 1990s, coffee jumped across the island chain, breaking new ground in flavors and growing techniques. Coffee now grows commercially on five islands in 10 regions.

Regardless of where or how it's grown, coffee is the world's drink. It seems that more people drink coffee than any other beverage except water and tea. In 2016, coffee was grown in 84 countries and imported into 195. Coffee fuels countless drinkers, getting them through each day, and maintains the livelihoods of people all over the world, from farmers to baristas.

If coffee is so ubiquitous, then what's so exciting about growing it in Hawai'i? For one thing, Hawai'i is the only state in the United States that grows appreciable amounts of coffee. This makes it easy to explore Hawai'i's coffee along every part of its journey—from bean to cup. In today's import/export market, this is a rare treat. In many countries, people don't drink the coffee they grow. In contrast, many of Hawai'i's farms play a big role in sharing their crop with local cafés, retail outlets and restaurants, and visitors can readily tour farms, enjoy a leisurely cup or purchase whole beans to take home.

Hawai'i's isolation and high cost of living have dissuaded farmers from competing in volume or price in the world market. Rather, Hawai'i's coffee industry competes by only producing high-quality, specialty coffee. Specialty coffee, sometimes known as gourmet or premium coffee, at the minimum, offers a clean cup full of coffeeness, though often it has distinctive flavors and unique characteristics. This is in contrast to canned and dehydrated coffees that are homogenous and have no outstanding traits. Every farm in Hawai'i has the potential to produce one-of-a-kind coffee.

Hawai'i's coffee industry has moved beyond just growing and selling coffee. Coffee has become an experience worth traveling for. In 2006, coffee farms were the dominate, specific agricultural farm type visited by agtourists (agricultural tourists). Since then, many more farms have opened their doors to visitors; some farms have even built visitor centers to support the experience. Farmers themselves are eager to meet people who want to learn about coffee. The whole state, not just the coffee industry, benefits when curious people explore the nature and culture of this fantastic crop.

People in the Hawai'i coffee industry are passionate, even fanatical. When talking to farmers, roasters or baristas, it's hard not to find their enthusiasm energizing. It's not just the caffeine that affects them. Coffee inspires minds, infuses dreams and fulfills destinies. For this industry, coffee isn't a way of life; it is life!

This book is meant to be a thorough exploration of coffee, from seed to cup. Certainly, it is meant to convey facts and figures and I think it does a decent job at that. However, I hope that it also helps you discover that every cup of coffee you drink should be worth thinking about. Whether you think about all the individuals who worked to create that cup, about the science and craft behind the cup or about the complexity of the taste, you should be aware that coffee is no longer simply a liquid caffeine delivery system—there's so much more there to appreciate and enjoy!

RIPE COFFEE AT MAUIGROWN COFFEE FARM,
KĀʻANAPALI, MAUI

CHAPTER 1
ORIGINS AND ISLANDS

A BRIEF HISTORY AND OVERVIEW OF HAWAI'I COFFEE

AS OF 2018, 7,200 acres of Hawai'i agriculture land were devoted to coffee. In 2012, coffee ranked second in the state for the largest amount of acreage devoted to a single crop (behind macadamia). In 2016, coffee was the second most valuable crop, second to seed crops, with a value of nearly $49 million (based on the price of coffee cherry). During the 2017–2018 season, Hawai'i's farms produced about 5 million pounds of green coffee, valued at about $86 million.

Coffee had a long, exciting history before making its way to Hawai'i. Coffee originates in Ethiopia and, originally, it wasn't consumed as a beverage. Some of the probably original uses include mixing the fruit (which also contains caffeine) with other ingredients to serve as an energy boost on journeys, using the fruit to make a tea, using the leaves to make a tea, and eating the roasted seeds like nuts. Once people began brewing it into a beverage, though, it didn't take long for it to make its way around the world.

Coffee arrived in Hawai'i on May 6, 1825, and was first planted in Mānoa Valley, on O'ahu. Chief Boki, the governor of O'ahu, is credited with a stop in Brazil aboard the HMS *Blonde* on a return trip from England to pick up coffee, amongst other plants. While those trees could be the parent plants of the industry, a possible introduction of plants from Manila shortly thereafter by Richard Charlton may hold that honor. The progenitor came to be known as 'Kanaka Koppe' and is now referred to as 'Old Hawaiian.' The missionary Samuel Ruggles introduced some of that original coffee to Hawai'i Island in 1828 or 1829. In 1836, the first commercial operation was planted in Kōloa, Kaua'i. Shortly thereafter, more than 1,000 acres of coffee were planted in Hanalei. Coffee then made its way around the islands. Of all these early commercial attempts, the only region that has remained in continual production to the present day is Kona, on Hawai'i Island.

In 1892, Hermann Weidemann, a sugar grower, introduced coffee from Guatemala in Hāmākua. It produced so much better than 'Kanaka Koppe' that growers in Kona planted it and called it 'Guatemalan Typica.' The name was changed locally to 'Kona Typica' in the 1990s to avoid confusing consumers. This is still the dominant variety planted in Hawai'i.

In the 1980s, when sugarcane and pineapple were in decline, several of the large fields were planted with coffee. Thus began the renewal of coffee farming across the entire state. Since then, coffee has moved into 10 major geographical regions on five different islands. In addition to these 10 regions, small farms can also be found across the state. Don't discount these lone farms; their isolation and lack of specific mention herein doesn't make them any less worthwhile or important to the industry.

If you're looking to experience Hawai'i's coffees, opportunities abound. To fully appreciate coffee, visit a farm to learn how it's grown from the ground up. You won't regret your emotional and intellectual attachment to this cherished crop. Most farmers look forward to meeting curious folk and teaching them all about coffee. While some farmers operate tour centers that welcome drop-ins, most farms prefer to arrange a private tour, by appointment only.

> ## WHAT IS A COFFEE ORIGIN?

An origin is defined by a region in which coffee is grown. The global industry has historically considered entire countries as regions. However, the definition has been changing to geographical areas within a country. Thus, you could buy coffee from Costa Rica or, more specifically, from the Tarrazú region. In Hawai'i, individual islands can be origins. With the expansion of coffee farming, though, origins are more commonly being referred to as regions within islands such as Kula or Ka'ū.

OTHER ORIGIN STORIES

There is confusion as to when coffee first
arrived in Hawai'i, evidenced by three dates
which can be found in use: January 21, 1813;
December 30, 1817 and May 6, 1825. The first two dates
are sourced from a translation of the journal of Don Francisco de
Paula Marín, an important contributor to Hawai'i's agriculture in
the early 1800s. The translation mentions "coffee" as one of the
many crops Marín was occupied with. However, the mention is
contained in a single commentary written in the margins of three
different pages that span a period of nearly 10 years covered by
the journal. The first two commentaries are found adjacent to the
journal entries for the first two dates listed above. Oddly, coffee
is not actually mentioned in any journal entry while many other
crops are. The commentary is written in the third person, which
suggests Marín did not write it, but that Robert Crichton Wyllie,
the translator, did.

Beginning with Wyllie and continuing through the 1980s, the
years 1813 and 1817 are used as arrival dates in reputable academic sources and by well-respected individuals and propagated
by any source wanting to list a date (the first edition of this book,
in fact, erroneously used the 1817 date). Unfortunately, aside
from that single commentary in the translation, there's no known
evidence that supports coffee's arrival or planting on either of
those dates.

Vasilii Golovnin, a Russian explorer, journaled about his meeting with Marín in 1818. He wrote, "The tireless Spaniard is making
efforts to obtain coffee trees and tea bushes, but so far has not
succeeded." Assuming the translation of this journal from Russian
is reasonably accurate, Marín couldn't have planted coffee on
either of the first dates because he hadn't yet obtained any!

Andrew Bloxam, a naturalist and a crew member on the HMS
Blonde, included an appendix in his journal that listed all the
plants brought to Hawai'i from Brazil; he listed 30 coffee plants.
The ship arrived at O'ahu on May 6, 1825.

KAUA'I

KAUAI COFFEE CO.

'ELE'ELE

KAUAI COFFEE COMPANY dominates the 'Ele'ele region and is the largest single-estate farm in Hawai'i, with more than 3,000 acres of coffee in production. A product of diversification from sugarcane, this farm began in 1987 and survived the enormous devastation of Hurricane 'Iniki in 1992 and the intense flooding of 2018. The entirely mechanized operation cares for more than seven different coffee varieties, with 'Yellow Catuai' accounting for 80 percent of trees.

Two other farms produce coffee on this island; they are small, family-owned operations.

HALE'IWA

Waialua

HONOLULU

O'AHU

WAIALUA

THE SINGLE FARM in this region is owned and operated by Dole Food Company Hawaii, of pineapple fame. Originally planted in the early 1990s with 'Kona Typica,' this orchard took a brief hiatus from coffee production but was renewed in 2006. Along with cacao (chocolate), this mechanically harvested farm is part of the company's crop diversification plan.

Small, experimental operations pop up occasionally across the island, though none has survived for very long. In recent years, the Hawai'i Agriculture Research Center has sold some of its crop commercially in an attempt to diversify its income stream for research.

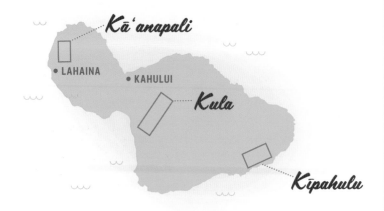

Kāʻanapali

LAHAINA

KAHULUI

Kula

Kīpahulu

MAUI

MAUIGROWN COFFEE

KĀʻANAPALI

MODERN COFFEE PRODUCTION began in this region in 1988 when Pioneer Mill Co. converted its sugar operation to coffee. Working closely with the University of Hawaiʻi, planters selected four different varieties to grow. The single farm here, MauiGrown Coffee, became famous for one of its varieties—the renowned 'Mokka.' It is still their most popular variety.

In the struggle between using land for agriculture or housing development, this farm embraced a clever solution. Within the actual farm, four-to-eight-acre, pre-planted coffee estates are available for residence, with one acre dedicated to the house itself and the rest planted in coffee owned by the homeowner but managed by the farm.

KULA

COFFEE HAS BEEN GROWN HERE for at least 30 years. There are probably 50 to 60 farms in this region. The coffee is grown along the leeward slopes of Haleakalā from 1,400-feet elevation to nearly 3,400 feet. Most plantings are probably 'Red Catuai' with other varieties scattered across many orchards.

KĪPAHULU

THE TWO FARMS HERE grow mostly 'Kona Typica,' certified organic, low-elevation (300 to 600 feet) coffee on the wet southeast coast. Much of the coffee is sold at roadside fruit stands although some of it makes it into high-end restaurants.

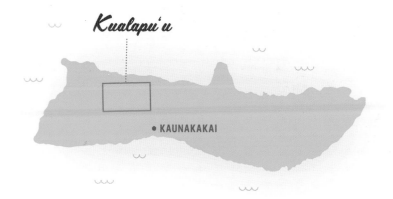

MOLOKAʻI
KUALAPUʻU

THE ONLY COMMERCIAL FARM HERE, planted in the late 1980s, is a large, mechanized operation owned by Coffees of Hawaiʻi. It mostly grows 'Red Catuai' and is known for its Muleskinner label, which is filled with fruit dried coffee.

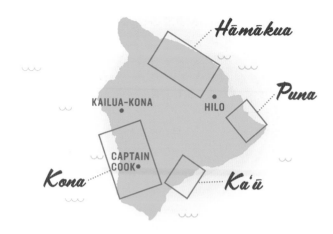

KAILUA-KONA

HILO

Hāmākua

Puna

CAPTAIN COOK

Kona

Ka'ū

BIG ISLAND

GREENWELL FARMS

KONA

COMPOSED OF 800 TO 900 FARMS ranging in elevation from 500 to 3,000 feet, this region defines Hawai'i coffee for most people. Kona coffee is internationally known and commands some of the highest prices in the world. Most farms are less than five acres in size and are operated by individual families. The variety 'Kona Typica' is grown almost exclusively here.

The early pioneers of Kona coffee were mostly English and German immigrants and Hawaiians. Henry Greenwell, an Englishman, produced coffee that was celebrated in Vienna in

1873. (Remarkably, his family still grows coffee in Kona today.) In 1892, Japanese immigrants disenchanted with life on sugar plantations began moving to Kona. Their passion and hard work maintained coffee production in Hawai'i, uninterrupted, since the first plantings in Kona. The region's reputation has long been held in high esteem. In the mid-20th century, with the help of University of Hawai'i scientists, this region boasted the largest coffee yields per acre in the world.

KA'Ū

THIS IS A RELATIVELY YOUNG REGION, having only resurrected in 1996 after the closing of the Ka'u Sugar Co. mill. Most growers here are part of a cooperative whose members each manage five to 12 acres. Because the cooperative does not have its own processing facility, most members have their coffee (mostly 'Typica') processed by a neighbor, a nearby mill or at mills in adjacent regions. Outside the cooperative, a few larger independent farms also exist. There are probably 80 to 90 farms here.

In the early years, Ka'u struggled with low prices and a poor reputation relative to its neighbor region, Kona. After a stunning competition debut at the 2007 Specialty Coffee Association of America's annual conference, Ka'u quickly garnered the attention of coffee buyers and consumers around the world. Currently, it commands prices similar to Kona coffees and is a highly respected region for its quality coffees.

RUSTY'S HAWAIIAN

PUNA

IN THE MIDDLE OF THE 19TH CENTURY, Puna hosted more than 6,000 acres of coffee. However, like most former coffee regions, it ceased coffee production with the rise of sugarcane. Farmers here mostly grow 'Red Caturra' but 'Kona Typica' can be found as well. This region is a high-rainfall, lava rock-based area ranging from 1,000 to 3,000 feet in elevation. Most of the more than 20 farms in this renewed growing region are about three to five acres.

BIG ISLAND COFFEE ROASTERS

HĀMĀKUA

IN 1852, Rev. Joseph Goodrich brought coffee to this region. Before long, more than eight plantations were established, the largest boasting over 1,000 acres. Fires and sugarcane quelled coffee production here until sugarcane production ceased in the mid-1990s. This region is a cool, high-rainfall, red soil-based coffee area that has now resumed coffee production with 'Kona Typica' and a sprinkling of other varieties. The average farm size is five to seven acres on elevations between 350 to 2,000 feet. There are probably about 15 to 20 farms here.

COFFEE VARIETIES IN HAWAI'I

IN HAWAI'I, all the coffee grown and sold for consumption is of the species *Coffea arabica*. While farmers use *Coffea liberica* 'Fukunaga' as the bottom half of a grafted plant to combat a root pest in some regions, it is never used as the top half. Within arabica, many varieties are planted throughout the world; Hawai'i grows a handful of them.

Unfortunately, historical records for variety introductions into Hawai'i are sparse, and the ones we do have are incomplete at best. Aside from the original introductions in 1825 and shortly thereafter, and the introduction from Guatemala in 1892, the next known introductions seemed to have occurred in the 1940s to 1960s. There is a confirmed introduction of varieties in 1954, though precisely who was responsible for it is not clear. Certainly, these three famous University of Hawai'i (UH) ag men, individually or as a group, were responsible: Eddie Fukunaga, Baron Goto and Richard Hamilton. There also may have been an introduction in 1982. The collection created by these gentlemen was planted at the UH experiment station in Kona, where many of the trees or their offspring still exist. Seeds from this collection were used to plant nearly all of the farms found in other Hawai'i coffee regions.

While the four large farms that were planted on old sugarcane land used seeds from the experiment station, three of them also brought in several varieties in the 1980s. In 1997, Skip Bittenbender introduced nine varieties from Brazil.

New varieties still arrive (see 'Geisha') and several large farms are actively seeking ways to bring in large numbers of plants of newer varieties. Coffee leaf rust is a devastating disease that is not yet in Hawai'i but is likely to make an appearance before too long. Thus, farmers are eager to introduce and test varieties known to be resistant to this disease.

Following are some varieties planted throughout the state. Some are quite common, while others might be found only on a single farm. The locations listed are for where the variety is most common, though it may be found elsewhere in small quantities.

Many factors will affect the taste profile of a variety; most notably, where they are grown and how they are processed and roasted. Thus, we'll avoid specific descriptions here. For more information on flavor, see the section on "A Quality Cup" beginning on page 57.

HAWAI'I-GROWN VARIETIES

BOURBON This variety, with 'Typica', are the two original varieties that spread around the world from Ethiopia via Yemen. The trees can be red, yellow or pink when ripe, giving us 'Red Bourbon', 'Yellow Bourbon' and 'Pink Bourbon'. It can be found on Hawai'i Island, Maui and O'ahu.

CATURRA This is a natural mutation of 'Bourbon'. It is a dwarf variety. The trees can be red or yellow when ripe, giving us 'Red Caturra' and 'Yellow Caturra'. It can be found on Hawai'i Island and Maui.

KAUA'I BLUE MOUNTAIN Found only on Kaua'i, this variety comes from the 'Typica' lineage.

CATUAI This is a cross between 'Caturra' and 'Mundo Novo'. It is a dwarf variety. The trees can be red or yellow when ripe, giving us 'Red Catuai' and 'Yellow Catuai'. It can be found on Hawai'i Island, Maui, Moloka'i and Kaua'i.

GEISHA This is a wild-type Ethiopian variety that has been made famous by a Panamanian farm. It is now the darling of the specialty coffee industry. Seeds were imported into Maui in 2010 by Greg and Susy Stille of Piliani Kope Farm and the seedlings were released from quarantine in April 2011. It can be found on Hawai'i Island.

MAMO This variety, available only in Hawai'i, is the only stable variety produced from a local breeding program. It is a cross between 'Maragogipe' and 'Mokka'. It can be found on Hawai'i Island.

MARAGOGIPE This is a natural mutation of 'Typica' that is a giant amongst varieties. Everything from the tree size to seed size is gigantic. It can be found on Hawai'i Island and Maui.

MUNDO NOVO This is a cross between 'Bourbon' and 'Typica.' It is a tall tree found mostly on Kaua'i.

TYPICA This is the variety that came from Brazil (1825), Manila (unverified introduction, shortly after 1825) and Guatemala (1892). Although 'Typica' is one variety, it is better understood as a lineage with variation, but not enough variation for individual lines to be unique varieties. The lineage from Guatemala was a more prolific producer than the previous introductions, which is why it came to dominate the farms in Kona. This is still the most common variety in Hawai'i and can be found on Hawai'i Island, Kaua'i, Maui, and O'ahu.

MOKKA This variety is more accurately called 'Tall Mokka.' It is a hybrid of true 'Mokka' and 'Typica' that was produced in Brazil. It is a dwarf variety, with everything on the plant being incredibly small. Due to its size, it is difficult to pick, thus, few farms on the planet grow it. It can be found on Maui.

SL28 This variety is from the 'Bourbon' lineage. It is not common in Hawai'i, but it is gaining attention. It can be found on Hawai'i Island and O'ahu.

FRESHLY PICKED COFEE CHERRIES AT MOUNTAIN THUNDER
COFFEE PLANTATION, KONA, HAWAI'I ISLAND

CHAPTER 2

THE PERFECT BEAN

GROWING, HARVESTING & PROCESSING COFFEE

WHO ARE HAWAI'I'S coffee growers? Are they estate owners who operate large plantations? Are they self-made farmers who toil on the land? Because Hawai'i is a very diverse state, it should come as no surprise that all kinds of people grow coffee, and that they do so using different types of agricultural and business models. Strategy aside, coffee farmers have one thing in common: They are passionate about their plants. The mystique and grandeur of coffee captures the growers' spirits. It builds a yearning that drives them to work for something beyond profits. They have a hunger for the land and love the labor of working with their well-cared-for plants.

Sole proprietors and families typically operate two to five acres of land, either owned or leased. They tend to maintain the farm on their income from it. Workers are often hired seasonally to pick all, or part, of the harvest.

Many of these farmers sell their freshly picked cherries to large processors. The processors then handle the coffee and sell the final product under their own label. Others hire someone to partly, or completely, process and roast the coffee. The farmers then sell the coffee under their own label. More complex small farms are vertically integrated; they grow their coffee and process the bean—all the way from raw to roasted—themselves, right on the farm.

Company-owned farms are the largest growers. With the cessation of sugarcane as a viable crop in the 1980s, many of the sugar-growing companies diversified into coffee production. These sizeable farms (more than 150 acres) are highly mechanized and completely integrated. Smaller company-owned farms exist, too. Generally around 20 to 150 acres, they harvest their coffee manually.

Because all of Hawai'i's farmers aim to grow high-quality coffee for the specialty market, they strive to take very good care of their fields. If the farm isn't too big, growers are often quite familiar with individual trees. Accordingly, each farm is uniquely cared for and maintained, as each farmer is a little different from the next.

Coffee is placed within the botanical family Rubiaceae, making it a close relative of gardenias and the tropical fruit noni. It has its own genus, *Coffea*, which contains 125 known species. Only two of these are commercially important: *Coffea arabica* and *Coffea canephora*.

C. arabica is recognized as the high-quality, high-value coffee. Nearly all specialty coffee is arabica. In fact, most of the coffee grown around the world is arabica. *C. canephora*, also known as robusta, is a hardier species with a less desirable taste.

Left unattended, arabica coffee can grow to be a 30-foot tree with a single, central stem. Lateral branches grow out at a 60- to 90-degree angle from this main stem. Leaves on each branch are paired and glossy. The flowers are white, smell a bit like jasmine and grow out of the nodes shared by a leaf pair. When the plants are in full bloom, the field looks as if it has just experienced a light snowfall. The flowers emanate a delightful, heady fragrance. Few crops beautify their farms as much as coffee.

Flowers and, consequently, fruit appear on each node only once. Thus, each season,

COFFEE IN BLOOM AT KUPA'A FARMS, KULA, MAUI (RIGHT) AND MOUNTAIN THUNDER, KONA, HAWAI'I ISLAND

as the branch grows longer, the older part of the branch serves mostly as support for the younger, productive part.

The part of the tree most important to us is the fruit. Botanically, the fruits are classified as drupes. Farmers call them cherries—as a matter of fact, true cherries are also classified as drupes, otherwise known as "stone fruit." Most coffee varieties, when ripe, are crimson in color. Other varieties, like 'Yellow Caturra,' 'Yellow Catuai' and 'Pink Bourbon,' have cherries with different colors, as described by their names.

We consume the seed of the fruit when we drink coffee. However, before we get to brew our favorite beverage, quite a bit of processing must be done. Subsequent chapters will elaborate on the processing. Right now, let's just stick to the fruit.

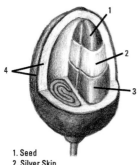

1. Seed
2. Silver Skin
3. Parchment with Mucilage
4. Skin and Pulp

SKIN AND PULP: This is the outermost layer and the only one that is actually fruity. It doesn't taste bad, but it doesn't exactly taste great, either. While it has plenty of

sugar and some caffeine, it also has a slight bitter taste. Dried cherry skin and pulp make an interesting herbal tea and was one of the first ways coffee was consumed by man.

....

"I love the fact that coffee starts off as a fruit. Most people don't get that. The fruit is sacrificed for the bean."

—Michelle Yamaguchi,
Waialua Estate Coffee & Chocolate

....

MUCILAGE: This is a liquid, sticky layer that surrounds the parchment and seed. It contains a bit of caffeine but, more importantly, it has a lot of sugar. It is nearly impossible to see ripe cherries and resist the temptation to squeeze some seeds into your mouth to suck on the tasty goo!

PARCHMENT: This layer is rough and papery. Before being shipped to an importer or roaster, coffee is typically stored with the parchment attached since it serves as a protective barrier. It must be removed before roasting.

SILVERSKIN: This layer is extremely thin and adheres tightly to the seed itself. Some processors polish it off before shipping the green coffee. However, this is unnecessary as it easily flakes off as chaff during roasting.

SEED: Called the bean or green bean when dry, the seed is hard and bluish-green in color. This is the part that is roasted into the brown coffee beans we know and love.

Nearly all coffee in Hawai'i is planted in hedgerows since this is agriculturally more efficient, although the older square pattern of planting can still be found. Some farmers simply let the coffee grow naturally and just harvest it every year, while others tend to it very intensively with irrigation, fertilization and weed control.

Generally, coffee farming in Hawai'i is sophisticated relative to other places that grow coffee. Advanced technology has arrived, proving Hawai'i as an innovator in coffee production. Notably, one large farm has installed water sensors in the soil throughout the farm that wirelessly transmit data for quick feedback on water availability for the crop. They also use drones with infrared cameras to help measure crop health, and they've installed cameras on their mechanical harvesters to give instant feedback to the operators, enabling them to make immediate changes to optimize the harvest.

Farmers prune their coffee trees regularly to facilitate easy management. With careful planning, tree heights are maintained at a reasonable level (usually less than 10 feet). Regular pruning also maintains high productivity. Pruning establishes multiple stems on each tree stump (normally three to five), instead of the single one that grows naturally when the tree is left unattended.

The older Kona-style pruning method allows farmers to choose a set number of vertical stems desired on each

A HEDGE PRUNER AT WAIALUA ESTATE COFFEE, NORTH SHORE, O'AHU

tree. Then, each year, they cut off the oldest stem and allow a new one to grow. In this system, the stems on the tree vary in age.

Alternatively, the Beaumont-Fukunaga method (named after the University of Hawai'i researchers who developed it in Kona), also known as stump pruning, cycles the number of vertical stems over time. Instead of having a single tree with multiple-aged stems, all the stems on a single tree are the same age. On rain-fed farms, entire rows are typically cycled on the same schedule, leaving rows of "different" ages, whereas on irrigated farms, pruning is done within a single irrigated section. Again, the farmer determines how many vertical stems will exist on each tree.

Pruning coffee requires a lot of time and labor. While it is a necessary farm activity in any orchard, local farmers seem to see it as more than just work. They recognize the importance of carefully shaping the future of the shrubs, tending to them as they would their children. This requisite attention fosters a connection between farmer and plants that inspires the pursuit of the highest possible quality.

Despite the farmers' TLC, pests and disease have the potential to endanger their crops. Critters such as microscopic bacteria and fruit-boring beetles eat the wood, roots, leaves or fruit. Until 2010, the pests and diseases found in Hawai'i, while a hindrance, were managed fairly

easily. The most notable of these critters are the green scale (*Coccus viridis*), the black twig borer (*Xylosandrus compactus*), the banana moth (*Opogona sacchari*), the Kona coffee root-knot nematode (*Meloidogyne konaensis*) and the Cercospora leaf spot/brown eyespot (*Cercospora coffeicola*). In 1888, King Kalākaua initiated the first quarantine on incoming coffee for the Hawaiian Islands. This quarantine (still in effect today), along with Hawai'i's geographical isolation, has played a major role in preventing the arrival of disastrous pests and diseases.

COFFEE BERRY BORER ENTERING A CHERRY (TOP) AND A BRANCH KILLED BY THE BLACK TWIG BORER

That changed in 2010 when the coffee berry borer (*Hypothenemus hampei*) arrived in Kona and steadily spread across the island and to two other islands. The tiny beetle enters a coffee fruit and bores a hole through the seed. There, it lays eggs. The female children eventually exit the fruit to infest new cherries. Left untended, the borer can destroy most of the coffee in a field. The beetle can be managed to levels of acceptable losses of seed, but it requires resources and diligence. Fortunately, Hawai'i farmers interested in controlling the population on their farm do so quite successfully.

A more recent addition to the pest scene is the little fire ant (*Wasmannia auropunctata*). While it does encourage unwanted green scale in a symbiotic relationship, its greater threat is to people—it has a nasty bite which can make hand harvesting untenable.

The average, healthy crop buds in the fall. After the requisite dry period ends with rain or irrigation, the majority of the flowers open for a few days, usually between January and March. Then, the waiting begins: the fruits take six to eight months to ripen. To frustrate matters further, the fruit won't necessarily all ripen at the same time, even if the flowers open on the same day. In wetter, high-elevation locations, farmers experience year-round flowering and, consequently, year-round harvesting. For most of the state, though, harvesting tends to begin in late August and lasts until January.

Due to the uneven ripening, a tree will have fruits with different degrees of ripeness. It is quite common to see immature, mature and overripe fruits simultaneously on a single branch. Farmers avoid harvesting immature fruits (also called underripes or green cherries) when possible, as they have a very poor taste. Farmers prefer to collect only ripe cherries, since they produce the best flavor. Overripe cherries also produce high-quality coffee, however, if they are exposed to moist environmental conditions, they tend to spoil. Since the overripes in drier areas are less likely to go bad, some farms harvest them and sell them as a unique product. In most cases, farmers simply visit each tree several times to ensure that they pick only the ripe ones, reducing waste.

Traditional hand picking is still the common harvesting method used around the state. When the fruits are ripe, family, friends and hired help (often foreign workers) don baskets and buckets and feverishly pick the choicest fruits one by one. When the

PICKING BY HAND AT KONA EARTH COFFEE, HAWAI'I ISLAND

IS COFFEE A TREE OR A SHRUB?

Depending on what you read, you'll see it called both. The difference between the two is just size and shape. A wild coffee plant will grow to be a tree. However, farmers keep their plants short and often prune them to establish multiple stems. So, in the field, coffee can be called a shrub. In everyday use, though, either term is ok.

MECHANICALLY HARVESTING AT KAUAI COFFEE COMPANY, 'ELE'ELE

basket is full, the cherries are dumped into a bag and set at the end of the row where they wait to be processed.

Hand picking is the quintessential coffee farming experience. No other activity helps a person better connect with the coffee plant. Furthermore, searching high and low for brilliantly colored cherries and weaving your hands between branches is a welcome reprieve from modern life. In fact, the undertaking can be almost meditative.

The four very large Hawai'i farms, however, have all given up on hand harvesting, save for the occasional cherry processing experiment. Labor

is expensive, and agricultural workers are scarce. Instead, they've championed mechanical harvesting.

Coffee-picking machines are redesigned blueberry harvesters. Since the operator must sit above the tops of the trees, the harvesting machines are quite large. As the harvester passes over the hedgerow, large columns outfitted with rotating fiberglass fingers knock cherries off the trees, indiscriminately of ripeness. The cherries fall onto a catch plate and are moved by a series of conveyors into a bin. The full bins are dumped and transferred to a truck to be taken to the wet mill.

Once enough cherries have been harvested, the processing begins; if cherries are left in bags or piles too long, they will overheat, decreasing the cup quality. Consequently, farmers try their best to process cherries the same day that they were harvested.

GERRY ROSS AND JANET SIMPSON

FARMERS

THINK BIG. GO LOCAL. This sums up the philosophy of Gerry Ross and Janet Simpson, the owners of Kupa'a Farms in Kula, Maui. The farm is a poster child for sustainable agriculture: everything is designed to produce food without compromising the ability of future generations to do the same. The farm produces a myriad of fruits and vegetables—one of its primary crops is certified organic coffee.

Gerry and Janet came to farming later in life while looking for new career paths. Gerry, a Connecticut native, was a research scientist for the Geological Survey of Canada but the work was losing its luster. Janet was already in the coffee business. She owned a coffee roastery and café in Calgary with her twin sister but was looking to move on to something new. In addition, her parents, who had 14 acres of land in Maui, were aging and thought having family around to help would be lovely.

At the start, they had no experience and no real intentions other than wanting to be organic and sustainable. To this end, they learned to divert as much organic waste as possible to their farm, use low tillage methods and incorporate shade trees. This has helped them improve soil health, reduce their carbon footprint, improve water retention in the soil and reduce reliance on out-of-state imports. Growing a diversity of crops, not just coffee, is an important part of sustainability as well. The diverse cropping system not only mimics the natural ecological environment, but it diversifies their income stream, letting them better handle any market shifts that might occur.

While they don't roast their own coffee currently, they do process it to green bean and have it roasted by a nearby roastery. Fortunately, they are able to sell nearly all their coffee as roasted product, thereby maximizing their profits on it as well. As a bonus, since they can work closely with their roaster, they can maintain control of the quality of the product that goes to their customers and into their cups. Like many farmers, they've found marketing their coffee to be a challenge, particularly because a fair price for a Hawai'i coffee is much higher than most restaurants and customers want it to be.

Farming coffee was never anything either Janet or Gerry ever expected to do. They tend to think coffee found them, rather than them finding coffee. Fortunately, they enjoy coffee and taking care of the earth and they are looking forward to working with both for a long time.

KUPA'A FARMS // 1886 Naalae Rd. // Kula, HI 96790 // www.kupaafarms.org
ⓞ : @kupaafarms

COFFEE PROCESSING

THE PURPOSE of coffee processing is to remove all the layers from the seed, dry the seed to a stable moisture content and prepare the coffee for sale. The first part of processing is wet milling. This is where the seed is dried and the layers are removed. Many farmers do the wet milling on their own farm, although it is also common for farmers to contract out this process to a nearby farm or large mill. The second stage is dry milling and it might occur some time after the wet milling. Very few farmers dry mill their own coffee, as the equipment tends to be large and too expensive for a small farmer to justify.

WET MILLING

There are myriad ways to extract the seed from the fruit and dry it down. Some methods remove the fruit first while others remove it last, after the seed is dried. No way is inherently better than any other. Every farmer will decide for themselves which method, or methods, they'll use. We won't explore all the possibilities here, just the ones most common in Hawai'i.

PARCHMENT DRIED

Also known as the wet method, the wet process, washed process and fermentation.

This is the most commonly used method for specialty coffee throughout the world, due in part to the long-standing belief that it produces better tasting coffee. This is dubious; other processing methods produce coffee that is just as good, only different. While this method still dominates in Hawai'i, the last few years have seen a proliferation of other methods and experimentation.

The first step involves removing and separating the pulp from the seed. Pulping requires little effort because ripe cherries easily give up their seeds. Most pulping operations have electric motors, though some small farms have hand crank machines.

The next step is to remove the mucilage, the sticky goo surrounding the seed. While its removal is not mandatory, if the coffee is going to be dried slowly in the open air, removal helps prevent growth of, or visits from, unwanted critters. To remove the mucilage, the coffee is often soaked in water. Large farms sometimes have elaborate tanks for this, while the smallest of farms just use

HAND CRANK PULPING MACHINE

WHEN IS A CHERRY RIPE?

Some say that the fruit must be monochromatic before it is ripe—that is, that the fruits must be completely red in red varieties and fully yellow in yellow varieties. Actually, the cherry is ripe when the seed easily falls out of the fruit when gently squeezed with fingers, which happens before the fruit becomes monochromatic. Nonetheless, it is commonly accepted that monochromatic fruits coincide with the greatest flavor potential for that seed.

plastic buckets. Farmers can also achieve the same effect by simply putting the pulped coffee in a container without water, where the mucilage removal occurs more rapidly. This water-free process is called dry fermenting (not to be confused with dry processing, which will be described in a moment!).

Regardless of the farmer's chosen method, the mucilage is removed by fermentation, which is carried out by microorganisms and is completed when the surface of the beans is no longer sticky. The time required for this varies depending on the temperature and, in Hawai'i, rarely takes longer than 10 hours. If the process is carried on for too long, the cup quality might decline.

For nearly the entire history of mucilage fermentation, it has been carried out by naturally present microorganisms. In the last few years, however, a handful of farmers have begun experimenting with spiking the fermentation tank with known yeasts, much as vintners and

bakers do. The effect of using a specific yeast on the cup quality is real, though apparently small. Nonetheless, the difference can be very important to farmers.

While fermentation is efficient at removing the mucilage, it requires substantial amounts of water and results in large quantities of dirty water to deal with afterwards. One solution to the water problem is to remove the mucilage mechanically.

JUST-PULPED SEEDS FALLING INTO A FERMENTATION TANK

TURNING COFFEE ON A HOSHIDANA AT GREENWELL FARMS, KONA, HAWAI'I ISLAND

Demucilaging technology is impressive; the amount of water used is less than 5 percent of traditional wet fermentation. Once the cherries are pulped, the beans are sent through a machine that rubs off the mucilage and then rinsed with minimal amounts of water.

After the demucilaging stage is complete, beans are rinsed and laid out on wood or concrete drying floors or trays where they will air-dry in two weeks or less. Several times a day they will be turned to speed up the drying process. In parts of Kona, the hoshidana, or drying rack, is still used. These Japanese-influenced drying decks have roofs that can be rolled away from the coffee to increase sun exposure. When rainy weather approaches, the roof is rolled back to shield the coffee. Other farms just cover their coffee with a plastic sheet.

The alternative to open air-drying is forced air-drying. While this method requires an extra financial burden of energy costs, it decreases the drying time to one to two days, allowing for more coffee to pass through the drying stage. When labor and maintenance costs are taken into account, forced air-drying can actually be cheaper than sun drying.

Drying is complete when the internal moisture content of the beans is 9 percent to 12 percent (by weight). This moisture level is the global standard. If you leave wet coffee to sun dry indefinitely, it will equilibrate to this level in most locations. Fortunately, this level of moisture is low enough to prevent most bacteria and fungi from being interested in the coffee.

At this point, the product is called parchment coffee. (The term "parchment dried"

FRUIT DRIED CHERRIES AT RUSTY'S HAWAIIAN, KA'Ū, HAWAI'I ISLAND

derives from the fact that when the coffee is drying, the parchment layer is exposed.) As mentioned earlier, the coffee is typically stored in this form until it is ready for roasting or shipment; parchment coffee is unroasted and it is not the coffee of commerce.

PULP DRIED

Also known as semi-washed, pulped natural and honey process.

This process is similar to the parchment dried method. The significant difference is that the mucilage is not removed from the seed before drying. Rather, it remains on the seed as a sticky mess. Depending on the amount of mucilage left on the beans and the drying conditions, the color of the mucilage will vary once dried; it can be yellow, red or black. Farmers mostly choose this process to affect the flavor of the coffee, as it often increases sweetness and adds complexity. However, as water isn't required for fermentation, it has a bonus of not requiring the farm to source fresh water and dispose of it after it is used.

FRUIT DRIED

Also known as natural process and dry process.

Essentially, pulping is skipped altogether and the coffee cherries are dried with their seeds still inside. Eventually, even within the cherry, the seed moisture content will reach the appropriate level.

There are two types of farmers who use this cherry processing method. Small farmers seeking to create a distinctive fruity cup are one group. The other group are farmers who harvest their coffee mechanically. If coffee cherries are left on the trees after they ripen (becoming overripes), they will eventually dry out. These dried cherries, also called "raisins," will be shaken off the tree during harvesting with the rest, separated and stored until the next stage of processing.

WET MILL QUALITY CONTROL

No matter how carefully cherries are picked, unwanted cherries, stones, leaves and sticks will find their way to the wet mill. Creating a spectacular cup of coffee means sorting out unwanted coffee and bits from the good stuff. This is particularly true with mechanically harvested coffee. In addition to the plant parts, a portion of the fruits that fall from the tree are underripes and overripes. In fact, it is this lack of selective harvesting that has given mechanical harvesting a bad reputation for coffee quality. In Hawai'i, all mechanically harvested operations intensively sort their coffee so that only the highest-quality beans are sold for consumption.

All pre-pulping separation occurs with water. Some cherries float, but most sink. The floaters either didn't develop properly, had only one mature seed (instead of two) or were overripe. When the floaters rise to the surface of a water-filled channel, they are easily routed away from the heavier cherries. The overripe cherries, if intended for consumption, will be sorted out in the dry mill (the next processing stage).

Once sorted, all the cherries are pushed through a machine with a slotted drum. The fleshy, ripe cherries get pulped and go through the

→ HOW IS COFFEE DECAFFEINATED?

Several solvents are used to remove caffeine from coffee. They all use unroasted coffee and, by law, must remove 97 percent of the original amount of caffeine in the bean before being sold in the US. None of the methods or solvents pose a human health risk. The most common solvents used to remove caffeine are water, supercritical carbon dioxide, methylene chloride and ethyl acetate.

Research laboratories have thus far been unable to produce genetically modified, caffeine-free plants, though several have tried. In 2004, Brazilian scientists announced the discovery of three arabica plants that produced virtually no caffeine. These natural mutants seem to lack the enzyme that converts theobromine, caffeine's molecular precursor in coffee, to caffeine. Using traditional breeding techniques, the research teams have been working to establish stable, agronomically desirable lines of high-quality, naturally decaffeinated coffee plants. It is an ongoing process.

DRY MILLING

While retaining the outer layers is a good way to store coffee, it cannot be roasted like that since those layers will catch on fire. (Nor will they taste very good!) Those layers are removed in a huller. Hullers remove the layers by rubbing the coffee against another surface like a rubber or metal plate or by beating the coffee with rotating rubber fingers. The coffee/layer mixture is then passed through a winnower which blows off the papery parchment. At this point, the coffee is called green coffee because it is mostly green in color (with a hint of blue hues).

All that now remains on the coffee seed is a very thin membrane called the silverskin. During roasting, the silverskin will harmlessly flake

TOP: DRY MILLING EQUIPMENT AT WAIALUA ESTATE COFFEE, NORTH SHORE, O'AHU. ABOVE: HAND SORTING COFFEE AT KEOKEA FARMS, UPCOUNTRY MAUI

slots while the underripes continue to move through the drum and out the other end.

On small farms, farmers may hand sort their cherries, ensuring only ripe and good-looking coffee moves forward through processing.

away from the coffee and can be evacuated from the roaster by steady airflow. However, as large volumes of green coffee will produce large volumes of chaff (cooked silverskin), some dry mills polish off the silverskin before sending the coffee away for roasting to reduce fire hazards.

DRY MILL QUALITY CONTROL

After hulling, and depending on the desires of the farmer, the green coffee is sorted through several different machines in order to increase uniformity of size and minimize the presence of defective or broken beans.

Typically, the first stage of sorting is done by size. The coffee is passed over screens with successively smaller holes. Beans that are smaller than the holes fall through while the larger beans stay on top. In Hawai'i, the holes are measured in 64ths of an inch, and only sizes 16 to 20 are typically used.

The coffee that falls through the size 16 screen is considered too small (coffee buyers like big beans). There are exceptions, however, that relate to the variety—'Mokka' is a notable deviation. Broken pieces, which also fall through, are unwanted because they do not roast evenly. The small and broken beans are sold as low-grade coffee, which might be used for extracting caffeine for anything from soda to pharmaceuticals.

Due to their shape, peaberries are separated out on the sizing screens, too. Peaberries, unlike typical coffee, lack a flat face. Instead, they are round like a pea. Most coffee cherries have two

COFFEE ON A GRADING SCREEN

seeds that develop inside. As they grow, they push against each other and form the flat face. When one seed fails to develop, the remaining seed grows small and round. All coffee plants produce a percentage of peaberries. In Hawai'i, this tends to be 5 percent to 8 percent of the green bean harvest, although there are some trees with up to 30 percent peaberries! Farmers who separate out the peaberries usually tout them as a rare and special product. There is debate over whether peaberries inherently taste different from their flat-faced brethren. In cases where a difference is detected, it could be an artifact of roasting; different shaped beans roast differently. A careful roaster can probably adjust the roast profile such that the different shaped seeds taste the same.

After the beans are sorted by size, they are taken to the gravity table where they are separated by density. A gravity table is slightly inclined in both the direction of flow and perpendicular to flow. While the table's surface vibrates, air is forced upward through its perforations. When uniformly sized green beans are passed over the table, the vibration and tilt cause the beans to separate by small changes (1 percent) in seed density.

After sorting on the density table, the coffee might finally be sent through a color sorting machine to pick out off-color beans.

COFFEE GRADING

The state of Hawai'i has strict regulations concerning how green coffee is labeled for sale. Various grades are defined to correlate to the appearance of the coffee. The grades differ mostly in the size of the beans, the number of defects per 10.6-ounce sample and the percentage of peaberries. In addition, the law protects the name of each region in Hawai'i. Therefore, certain rules must be obeyed if a label is to include a specific origin like "Kona" or "Maui."

Many farms do not sort and grade their coffee to the fullest extent possible. Instead, they clean their coffee to a respectable level and sell it as roasted product without a certified grade. Some will label this "estate" coffee. Typically, these are small farms with such small volumes of coffee that separating their coffee by size, density and color is impractical.

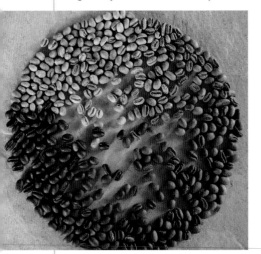

PEABERRY COFFEE AT VARYING ROAST LEVELS

COFFEE QUIZ & FUN FACTS

Will coffee dehydrate you? We all know that coffee (caffeine, really) is a mild diuretic. Interestingly, our bodies replace the water we lose, even during exercise, with the water in the coffee. Consequently, drinking coffee does not create a net loss of water.

Is coffee bad for you? For most people, coffee is a safe and, oftentimes, therapeutic drink. In fact, most research shows that coffee may be good for us! Most of the negative impacts from coffee are associated with sensitivity to caffeine, not with coffee specifically. If caffeine is problematic, drinking decaf will likely be a solution.

Coffee Factoids

These numbers are based on the coffee/water ratio of .44 oz./8 oz. The ranges occur due to bean size, bean density and roast level.

Beans per pound: 2,800 to 4,725
Beans per cup: 80 to 135
Cups per pound: 36
Cost per cup: $1.24/8 oz. cup (at $45/roasted pound)

ROASTING AT HAWAI'I COFFEE COMPANY,
HONOLULU, O'AHU

CHAPTER 3
THE ART AND SCIENCE OF ROASTING
PROCESS, FLAVORS & BLENDS

COFFEE ISN'T "COFFEE" until it is roasted. This process converts a somewhat inert seed into a complex bean composed of more than 1,500 different chemicals. Arguably, coffee is the most chemically complex food humans consume.

The process of roasting coffee isn't much different than popping popcorn—and, in fact, you can use a popcorn popper to do it! Heat is applied to the beans for eight to 15 minutes, depending on the desire of the roaster. In the process, the bean goes through complicated chemical changes that turn it from green to straw-yellow to tan. After tan, the hue deepens until it reaches black. During the course of the roast, the bean will pop at least once. (As with popcorn, this is the sound of cells breaking from water vaporizing.) During longer roasts, a second popping will occur. (This time, when carbon dioxide and other gasses escape from the cells.)

There are two basic types of coffee roasting machines. Each influences the taste of the coffee, and most roasters feel strongly about the type of machine they use. The most common type is the drum roaster. It works by conducting heat from a flame or electric coil to a rotating metal drum that contains the coffee. The other type is the air roaster. This machine uses the convective force of rapidly moving hot air to transfer heat to the beans.

COFFEE ROAST GRADIENT, FROM UNROASTED GREEN TO DARK ROAST

Roasting is a craft. Each coffee must be nurtured carefully to extract its greatest flavor potential. The roaster can manipulate the length of the roast, temperatures at various stages during the roast and the end color of the roasted bean. The choices of all these factors comprise the roast profile. The roast profile will determine the final taste of the coffee.

Roast level has a huge influence on coffee taste. A single coffee roasted to different degrees of darkness can sometimes seem unrelated. As coffees are roasted darker, predictable changes occur.

Lighter roast coffees, if inherent to the bean, have higher taste-acidity and permit interesting, nuanced flavors to be detected. Medium roast beans have fewer nuances and more body. Darker beans have even more body, fewer nuances, bitterness and tend to have smoky, woody or char notes.

The unique, positive characteristics of a coffee are most noticeable at lighter roasts, as are off-flavors. Roasting a coffee darker can mask some of those flavors. Darker roasts also allow more coffee flavor to be expressed when milk and sugar are used.

Many coffee roasters retail their beans in their own shops, at farmer's markets, in local stores, via the internet or, if they are also farmers, right off the farm. Consequently, they tend to care a great deal about product quality.

While most local coffees roasted in Hawai'i come from a single region or single farm, part of the artistry in coffee roasting is blending coffees of various origins. Some roasters create blends composed entirely of different Hawai'i coffees while others import beans from around the world to use in their special blends.

→ WHAT IS "STRONG" COFFEE?

Technically, coffee strength refers to how much extracted coffee is in the brew in relation to how much water is in the cup, a value largely determined by the ratio of water to coffee used during brewing, though many other brew factors can play a roll. Coffee strength is a continuum, with "weak" being on the other end. However, the term "strong coffee" is used in all sorts of other ways by all sorts of people.

People use "strong" to refer to their experience of the roast level (darker roasts being described as stronger), the intensity of the bitterness (more bitter described as stronger), the caffeine content (more caffeine described as stronger) or the overall intensity of the taste (though people can never seem to be specific about what this means). Since there are so many different meanings for "strong coffee," be sure to figure out exactly what a person means if they use it!

TOP: A ROAST LOG DOCUMENTS TEMPERATURE, TIME AND OTHER DETAILS. ABOVE: STEPHEN JAMES DAVIDSON ON CHECKS THE ROAST PROGRESS.

By blending, a roaster mixes flavors to create entirely new experiences. Many roasters blend to find a coffee flavor that nobody else has, thereby creating a unique product. They may create a blend that works particularly well for a specific brew method. A roaster may also blend a more expensive coffee with a cheaper one to capture its flavor while making it more affordable. Also, if a particular coffee has a revered reputation, it may be used in a blend so that its name can be used for marketing, such as "Kona."

It may be surprising that roasters import green coffee to Hawai'i for roasting since we grow plenty of it ourselves! Unfortunately, we probably don't grow enough coffee to satisfy demand for residents and visitors alike.

Additionally, Hawaiian coffee is expensive for residents, too; not everyone can afford to drink it every day.

In line with King Kalākaua's first quarantine (page 23), not just any green coffee can be imported to the Islands. After all, there is a chance that unwanted pests and diseases could hitch a ride on green coffee grown elsewhere. Thus, only green coffee that has been appropriately treated prior to arrival in Hawai'i is allowed to be imported legally. While there are several approved treatments, such as roasting and freezing, only one is actually used: fumigation.

The fumigation occurs at the green coffee's penultimate destination, typically a port in California. The chemical used for fumigation is methyl bromide. Once a commonly used chemical for pest control in soils and buildings, it has largely been phased out of use in the US as it is an antagonist to the ozone layer and is toxic to aquatic organisms. However, it is permitted for select uses; treating coffee for the Hawaiian Islands is one of them. Methyl bromide is very volatile, so it likely is not present in the green beans once they depart for Hawai'i and any that might remain will evaporate during the roasting process.

The fumigation doesn't impact the coffee in any way. There is no apparent taste change and the roasting of the coffee isn't impacted. Fumigation with methyl

> "To truly appreciate a good cup of coffee, drinkers need to be aware of what the coffee bean goes through when processed. The poor bean is burned by roasting, ground in a grinder, only to have hot water poured over it. One could easily conclude that the lowly coffee bean literally goes to hell and back in order to reach our palate."
>
> —Michael Conway,
> Dole Food Company Hawaii and
> Waialua Estate Coffee & Chocolate

bromide does, however, contradict organic certification, thus no unroasted coffees that arrive from elsewhere can be labeled organic.

One giant exception to green coffees permissible for import is African coffees. No green coffee of African origin is allowed to be imported under any condition. The reason for this is that coffee berry disease (*Colletotrichum kahawae*), a fungal disease still restricted to the African continent, was once thought to be systemic, even residing in green beans. Thus, to protect our industry from this disease, a complete ban was written into law. We now know that coffee berry disease is not systemic and the risk of it arriving on or in green beans is miniscule. Nonetheless, the law still exists.

FRED HOKADA

ROASTER AND CAFÉ OWNER

FRED HOKADA was born and raised in Honolulu. Aside from his college years, he has always lived in Hawai'i. After college, he worked in information technology, helped take care of his ailing mother and ended up working in a local coffee shop in Waikīkī. As it turned out, he discovered specialty coffee, the language of coffee, coffee people and coffee worth standing in line for. When a friend decided to move away and sell his small roastery and café in 2010, Fred decided it was time to own his own business and purchased Downtown Coffee Honolulu.

At the time, Fred didn't know how to roast coffee but he knew he could learn it. He also knew he could imprint his own personality to the café and continue to grow its customer base. Since taking ownership, Fred has made Downtown Coffee Honolulu a beloved presence in the heart of downtown Honolulu.

It is rare for a café to also roast its own coffee. Fred has not only maintained this practice but expanded his house-roasted coffee inventory. More importantly, he decided early on to roast and serve only Hawai'i-grown coffees.

At first, it just seemed easier to buy from local farms rather than a mainland supplier. In a short amount of time, however, Fred discovered immense satisfaction in supplying reasonably priced cups of locally grown coffee to his customers, especially brewed as espresso. It all just made sense— Hawai'i coffee is special because Hawai'i is his home. Hawai'i has great people and great stories which help produce great coffee. Why would he want to serve coffee grown anywhere else?

Fred has entrenched himself in the local coffee industry. He can be found at every coffee-related competition on O'ahu, he sponsors coffee events, he visits other cafés whenever he has a spare moment and he drinks any coffee he can get his hands on. Moreover, there isn't a person in the coffee world that doesn't think Fred is a friendly, genuine, delightful person.

Fred is so enmeshed in the coffee industry because coffee inspires Fred. More accurately, the idea that coffee is different for everybody inspires him. Everyone has their own opinions about coffee: how it tastes or how it should be enjoyed or what one should be drinking... That's ok. There's no right answer. Thus, you can learn something about coffee from anyone. Inspiring.

DOWNTOWN COFFEE HONOLULU // Pioneer Plaza, Ground Floor // 900 Fort Street Mall, #100 // Honolulu, HI 96813 // www.dtcoffee.com // 📷 : @dtcoffeehonolulu

HAWAI'I COFFEE AND BLENDS

WHILE ANY HAWAI'I-GROWN coffee can be blended, typically only Kona coffee is used, and the blends only contain 10 percent Kona coffee. The use and marketing of these 10 percent Kona blends is controversial. The core of the issue is whether a product where only 10 percent of its contents come from a certain place should be able to use the name of that place in its name. At the same time, more Kona coffee is probably sold as part of a blend rather than as a 100 percent product, implying that consumers are satisfied and the problem is more of an academic and philosophical issue, considering that from a financial perspective the increased sales do more good for the market as a whole. The issue is complex and has no simple solution. The discussion is political, economic and social.

Legally, a Hawai'i roaster can use the name of a Hawai'i origin on a roasted bag of coffee if the bag contains at least 10 percent, by weight, of that origin. While the content can be greater, few roasters use more than 10 percent and they almost always use coffee from the Kona region. Much lower-priced world coffees comprise the remainder of the blend. These blends exist because consumers want access to Kona coffee but they choose not to purchase 100 percent Kona coffee, likely because the cost is relatively high.

COFFEE PLANTS FLOWER MULTIPLE TIMES, PRODUCING FRUITS THAT RIPEN OVER MANY MONTHS. HARVESTING (USUALLY BY HAND) REQUIRES MULTIPLE VISITS TO THE SAME TREE, AND THUS HIGHER COSTS FOR THE FARMER AND BUYER. HERE, THE COFFEE IS FLOWERING WHILE FRUIT IS READY TO BE PICKED, AN ESPECIALLY DIFFICULT SITUATION.

Consumers want these blends. Every grocery store, drug store and tourist-centered shop in Hawai'i carries them, often in multiple variations. The high demand means they are a successful product for the roasters to offer and have been for decades.

Moreover, most farmers likely benefit from these blends. Unfortunately, there are no data that tells us how much Kona coffee actually gets blended. Conservatively, I estimate it to be at least 55 percent of all Kona coffee. More striking is my estimate that 80 percent of farmers have at least some coffee that ends up in blends, as many estate farmers tend to sell a small bit of coffee cherry to processing mills that sell coffee to the roasters who make these blends.

→ WHAT IS A FLAVOR PROFILE?

The experience of drinking coffee can be broken down into individual components. As you'll read later, these include factors such as acidity and aroma. In addition, coffees can have unique tastes and nuances that don't appear in every brew. The collective experience of all these different parts is the flavor profile.

"The 'perfect' cup is the experience of an extremely rare consonance of innumerable factors coming together over great distances of space and time."

—Brandon Damitz,
Big Island Coffee Roasters

Economically, it seems to be a win-win for everybody. So, why are people against these blends? There are four main reasons.

First, ethically, using the name "Kona" when only a tiny bit of the product actually contains coffee from this place is rather murky. Moreover, the other 90 percent of the blend is barely, if at all, mentioned, meaning the 10 percent is a mere token amount used just to grab customers' attention with the name "Kona." In other words, it is a cheap marketing trick.

An ironic counter spin to the marketing angle is that the marketing of these blends might actually promote bags that contain 100 percent Kona coffee. If a bag that is just 10 percent Kona coffee tastes good and is worth buying, then the implication is that a bag that is all Kona coffee must be amazing. The blends may inspire the occasional splurge on a 100 percent Hawai'i-grown coffee.

Quality brings us to the second point. A blend that contains only 10 percent Kona

COFFEE FIELDS AT KAUAI COFFEE COMPANY IN 'ELE'ELE, KAUA'I

coffee may not represent the taste of Kona coffee—or worse, might be lackluster or even terrible. This is certainly the belief of many 100 percent-Kona coffee advocates. Consumers then associate this lower-quality coffee with Kona and begin to believe Kona coffee is not good at all. This is the third reason for protest: damaging Kona's reputation. Over time, then, consumers may turn away from Kona coffee, thereby hurting the industry at large.

Folks who disagree with the minimum percentage of 10 advocate for all coffee in Hawai'i that designates an origin only contain that origin. As that seems unlikely ever to come to pass, alternative percentages have been mooted as compromises, namely 75 percent—to match California wine rules—and 51 percent—so at least most of the bag's contents comes from that origin.

Everyone who sells Kona coffee in Hawai'i would love to sell it as only pure Kona coffee. However, many people just don't think that is feasible and the consequences of forcing that percentage could be intense. If the law were changed to force a higher percentage of the blend, prices for the blends would increase and many customers might move to other, moderately priced coffees. If this happened, the supply of Kona would likely increase and green bean prices would probably crash. The effects would be felt not just by retailers, but by farmers who no longer have an outlet for their coffee as the new prices would be unsustainable for them and

→ WHAT IS THE HAWAI'I-GROWN COFFEE LAW?

This law aims to protect Hawai'i coffees sold in Hawai'i from being misrepresented in blends. (The law does not apply to coffee sold outside of the Hawaiian Islands.) It mandates that if a Hawai'i coffee is used in a blend and is named on the package, then the package must represent the coffee accurately. Not only must the blend contain at least 10 percent (by weight) of the origin named, but the label must also clearly state the percentage, and the size of the font on the label must adhere to specific guidelines.

still probably not low enough to encourage purchase of the pure coffee by consumers.

This scenario is speculative, but Hawai'i lawmakers are hesitant to make any changes as they may cause more harm than good. Everyone agrees marketing research could help determine what might happen, but nobody has yet offered to foot the bill.

In recent years, bills have come up in the legislature aimed at changing the blend percentage. While it seems like the idea is gaining support, nothing has been successful. In the meantime, consumers have the power to choose whichever coffee they want. Perhaps the solution to this controversy is to educate, not legislate.

Currently, existing legislation protects roasted Hawai'i coffees when they are used in blends. Nonetheless, the law doesn't appease everyone. To learn more about the blend controversy, see "The Kona Kai Scandal" sidebar on page 107.

KIMO FALCONER OF MAUIGROWN COFFEE INSPECTS RECENTLY HARVESTED FRUIT DRIED COFFEE

CHAPTER 4
COFFEE CONSUMPTION
TASTING, GRINDING, & BREWING

FINALLY, we've reached the part where we get to talk about drinking, tasting and knowing coffee! Coffee fulfills different needs and desires for different people. For some, it is merely a way to jump-start the day. For others, a coffee break is an excuse to socialize with co-workers or friends. For a quickly expanding group of people, however, drinking coffee is an exercise in deconstructing a complex experience and exploring it on a physical, emotional, social and intellectual level.

We tend to think of taste as something that happens automatically when food or drink reaches our taste buds. It isn't that simple. Whether we realize it or not, taste is a multifaceted process that involves our brains as much as our mouths—an amalgamation of social and cultural contexts, emotion and, of course, the physical response to foods or beverages. By considering each of these aspects—separately and collectively—we can gain a sophisticated appreciation for tastes and flavors. This same process works for all complex comestibles such as wine, single malt scotch, cheese, chocolate and, naturally, coffee.

In many ways, coffee appreciation emulates wine connoisseurship. Like wine bottles, coffee bags don labels detailing the beans' unique flavor, regions and farm names. And in some cases, coffee prices are beginning to track people's perception of beans' quality.

WHAT DOES "ORGANOLEPTIC" MEAN?

"Of, relating to, or involving the use of sense organs or senses, especially of smell and taste," according to the *Oxford English Dictionary.* "Organoleptic" denotes the entire physical experience of consuming something, not just how it tastes. It is used by many groups of people, including anthropologists and food scientists.

To understand tasting (rather than drinking), you should begin with its organoleptic qualities. Although not part of the English vernacular, "organoleptic" is used here for two reasons. One, it is important to discern this measure of coffee quality from other types of quality, such as bean size, density and defects. Two, the experience of coffee includes not just taste, but other senses, too.

Unfortunately, assessing quality is not easy. One important reason for this is that we rarely ever just sit and think about the coffee. We are normally too distracted by the world around us.

In a way, we have a social relationship with coffee. It accompanies our breakfast and midday breaks, it joins us at meetings with friends and colleagues and it is inextricably linked with our cultural framework. It isn't that we can't assess quality in all these situations; rather, we just don't have any practice doing it. Removing the social context from coffee consumption allows us to more easily assess quality and, in fact, explore our social interaction with this beverage.

Most people have a fairly simple experience of coffee. They expect it to taste like coffee and not have any unpleasant flavors. Unfortunately, this simplistic model does not facilitate useful communication about coffee quality; the specialty coffees now available are too complex to be comprehensively described this way. This oversimplification also limits the potential experience one can have with the coffee.

The biggest mistake people make when discussing organoleptic quality is confusing it with preference, which is subjective. Conversely, quality is objective. At least, it is once it's defined. Whether you like a coffee or not says very little about its quality. There's nothing wrong with a subjective experience of coffee—you should like what you drink. However, liking something is different than discovering what it is.

Over the course of many decades, the coffee community—traditionally green coffee buyers and government regulators—has created a framework with which to discuss quality. They have selected characteristics that the group deems worth having or worth avoiding and have created

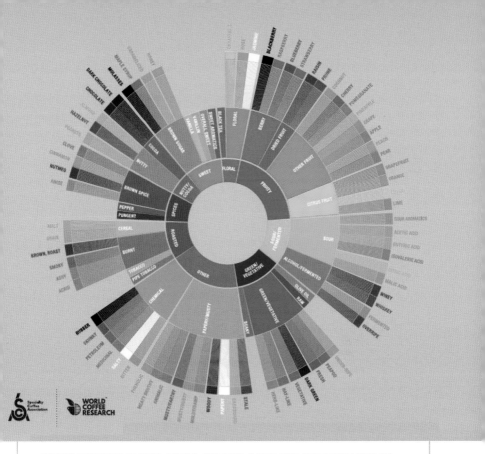

COFFEE TASTER'S FLAVOR WHEEL CREATED USING THE SENSORY LEXICON DEVELOPED BY WORLD COFFEE RESEARCH

a vocabulary with which to discuss them. While the decision of which characteristics to choose can be subjective, the analysis of them can be objective. As everyday coffee drinkers develop their tasting palates, they will ultimately become the arbiters of quality.

When sampling coffee, tasters typically discuss six main characteristics: aroma, body, flavor/coffeeness, acidity, sweetness and aftertaste. These can be thought of as the backbone of a coffee and every coffee can be explored in these terms.

There is an extensive number of additional descriptors that, because they will not be found in every cup, truly set coffees apart from each other. These include flavors seemingly unrelated to coffee— such as caramel, lemon and nuttiness—and undesirable off-flavors—like medicinal, rubber and sour.

Once the basic characteristics are defined, you can discuss their intensity. Are they completely absent (not intense) or are they so present that no other coffee could have a greater level of that experience (very intense)? When taste testing, try to define the coffee based on what is present in the cup (quality), not how much you like it (preference).

COFFEE CHARACTERISTICS

Different evaluation systems score these characteristics differently. They can be rated entirely on intensity, where the rating scale ranges from not intense (not present) to very intense (very present). Alternatively, they can be scored on a blend of intensity and preference. (See the scoring worksheet in the Resources section.)

AROMA The smell of coffee is distinctive, both when the coffee is just dry grounds and also after it has been brewed. Evaluating the aroma allows us to pick up on freshness and off-flavors. It also suggests the roast level and, perhaps, some taste descriptors.

BODY This is a tactile descriptor. It describes how viscous or heavy the coffee feels in our mouths. A good analogy is to think about how skim milk feels differently from whole milk in your mouth.

COFFEENESS This is the essence of the cup, the paradigm of the coffee flavor experience. How much does it taste like what coffee should taste like? This is the most challenging of the characteristics because it requires a plethora of experiences to draw upon in order to be accurate. "Coffeeness" is not a recognized term, in fact, I only recently began using it. Typically, cuppers use "flavor" instead.

ACIDITY Most coffee has some amount of acidity. It is best understood as the bright, lively, tingly sensation experienced with fruits, like citrus and apples.

SWEETNESS This is a subtle experience that reminds us of the taste we associate with sucrose (table sugar). Comparing this sensation to a known sweetness is difficult; nonetheless, the sensation is distinctly sweet.

AFTERTASTE This refers to the coffeeness perceived in the mouth after the coffee has been expectorated or swallowed.

Assessing quality initially is more valuable than assessing preference for two reasons. First of all, it is impossible to discuss a coffee with another person if you only use ideas that are true for you. More importantly, compartmentalizing a coffee's quality will permit you to discover why you like the coffee. This insight will give depth to your coffee experience and empower you to explore the experience emotionally and intellectually.

Coffee tasters, like wine connoisseurs, have a formal method of assessing coffee quality, called cupping. People who assess coffee using this format are called cuppers. Everyone can cup coffee—and everyone should! Becoming a skilled cupper is difficult; fortunately, experience and practice go a long way toward perfecting one's skills.

There are two major reasons to cup coffee. First, it eliminates emotional and social contexts. It is difficult to analyze a cup of coffee when you're sitting at the breakfast table, newspaper in hand, with the idea of work looming ahead. The cupping format creates a new context that, with a standardized vocabulary and protocol, allows you to use your body as an instrument for objective analysis.

The second major reason we cup is because anyone, anywhere can do it. It requires no fancy equipment, no special conditions and no educational degree. Using hot water, ground coffee, cups

and spoons, a cupper can have the same cupping experience in Hawaiʻi as someone in Ireland or Ethiopia. There is no worry about how different coffee pots will affect the brew or if the brewing temperature is high enough. All the conditions for making the coffee can be standardized, from how much coffee is used to the water temperature. With standardization, we can have a conversation about the same thing: quality.

MARIO ROMERO PREPARES COFFEE USING A CHEMEX BREWER

....

"Oh, how sweetly tastes the coffee, more lovely than a thousand kisses, milder yet than Muscatel. Coffee, coffee I must have, and if someone wants to please me then pour coffee in my cup."

—Johann Sebastian Bach from *Kaffee-Kantate*, BWV 211 (translated by Clive Williams)

....

HOW TO BREW A GOOD CUP OF COFFEE

SOURCE HIGH-QUALITY COFFEE. Finding high-quality coffee requires finding a roaster you trust. Whether you buy locally or online, many excellent roasters exist to serve your needs.

USE ONLY FRESH COFFEE. If you're drinking for flavor, stale coffee isn't worth drinking. If you don't know when the coffee was roasted, don't buy it. Most coffee drinkers can probably detect staling coffee about a month after it's roasted.

GRIND THE COFFEE TO THE APPROPRIATE SIZE WHEN YOU NEED IT. Different brew methods require different grind sizes. Know what your method needs. Also, ground coffee stales much quicker than whole bean coffee. Grind it just before you are planning to use it.

BREW COFFEE TO THE RECOMMENDED STRENGTH. The Specialty Coffee Association recommends using 13 g coffee/236 ml water (.44 oz./8 oz.) for most brewing methods. Start here and adjust as necessary to suit your taste.

USE CLEAN WATER. Since brewed coffee is 95 to 98 percent water, using bad water will produce bad coffee. If your tap water tastes bad, use filtered water.

USE WATER HEATED TO THE PROPER TEMPERATURE. Most brewing methods require water to be 195–205° F.

DRINK THE COFFEE AT A TEMPERATURE THAT WORKS BEST FOR YOU. However, don't let the coffee sit on a heater for more than 15 minutes—constant heat causes important flavor components to be lost. Don't be afraid to drink it at different temperatures. Cold coffee can be very good. Don't reheat coffee using any method. Reheating coffee diminishes the positive characteristics.

DRINK IT HOW YOU LIKE IT. High-quality coffee is usually very tasty by itself. If you normally use a whitener and/or sweetener, sip the coffee black a few times before making any additions. If it isn't for you, go ahead and make it the way you like it.

PREFERENCE IS SUBJECTIVE. Drinking coffee is supposed to be a pleasure. Thus, all coffee "rules" and expert opinions should be broken to suit your taste!

A CUPPING SESSION IS THE BEST WAY TO APPRECIATE COFFEE'S COMPLEXITIES

HOW TO CUP

The best way to understand and appreciate cupping is to do it. Sharing the experience with friends will make it more fun and discussing it will improve your understanding of the coffee. Don't be surprised if the first few times don't go very smoothly. Be patient. Slurping coffee from a spoon and thinking about it takes practice.

Begin by filling all the cups with dry, ground coffee.(See sidebar on page 54 for details on preparing for a cupping.) If you can, have someone do this for you. The less you know about the coffee, the less biased you'll be. Cuppers use different formats, even different recording systems, for their cupping. Each has its own merits and detractions. The following procedure is the method I use.

Once the cupping table is set, gently shake the cup of dry, loose coffee to stir up the aromas trapped beneath the surface. Then, deeply inhale the aroma. Most cuppers put their noses in the cup to improve their smelling. After the aroma intensity has been assessed for each coffee, add hot water and mark the time.

The coffee will float to the surface of the cup, forming a crust. After four minutes of brewing, use a spoon to break the crust.

If you smell the coffee precisely while breaking the crust, you'll detect an unpleasant, chemically aroma. Don't worry—this is normal. After a second or two, the scents you associate with coffee will begin to escape from the cup. At this moment, assess the wet aroma.

While the coffee cools, clean up the cup of brew (it helps to use two spoons to corral the grounds). Some of the coffee will sink conveniently

MATERIALS FOR CUPPING

1. A deep, rounded spoon, like a soup spoon

2. A wide-rimmed cup or bowl that holds 5 to 6 ounces of water

3. 0.29 ounces of medium-coarse ground coffee

4. 5 ounces water (at ~200°F)

5. A cup of water for rinsing the spoon after each cup

6. A spittoon for spitting

7. A score sheet to rate characteristics and make comments (see Resources)

8. A clock that measures seconds

9. A cup of water or neutral food (plain bread or crackers) for clearing your palate between samples (optional)

These amounts of coffee and water are not absolute. Any ratio will work as long as you define it and remain consistent. These numbers are based on the Specialty Coffee Association's recommended brew strength of 7.3 ounces of coffee per 1 gallon of water.

to the bottom of the cup after the crust is broken. However, the coffee remaining on the surface must be scraped away to make tasting it easier. After all, who wants to taste, or even feel, coffee grounds?

Once the coffee is cool enough to drink, about six or seven minutes from the initial pour, the tasting can begin. Use the spoon to bring the brew to your mouth. Neither sip nor swallow it. To ingest the coffee, vigorously slurp from the spoon! The primary idea is to spray the coffee evenly over the mouth so that all your taste buds will come into contact with the coffee simultaneously. After a few seconds (and some swishing around if so desired), spit the coffee out. After spitting, rate the characteristics, beginning with acidity.

Most of the characteristics are stable and do not change during the course of the cupping. This is not true for acidity. As the coffee cools, the acidity will increase. Therefore, the acidity for all the cups should be evaluated at the same brew temperature. Don't worry about using a thermometer. Simply rate the acidity for each cup at about the same time after having added water. If cupping several coffees at once, it will help to begin brewing the coffees in 30-second intervals. In addition, because coffee grounds always remain in the cup, the coffee is continuously brewing. To avoid overextraction, the assessment of a single coffee should not exceed 10 to 11 minutes in total time.

A CUPPER BREAKS THE CRUST AND ASSESSES AROMA

Part of the difficulty in assessing quality is knowing the scale of intensity. The absence of a characteristic is easy to detect. However, determining a maximum intensity is more difficult. Unless you have been specifically trained, you will have to rely upon experience. As you cup more and more coffees from a diversity of origins, you'll begin to learn the maximum intensities for each characteristic. Alternatively, you can make use of World Coffee Research's Sensory Lexicon (see page 49, also available online). It offers definitions of many quality terms and standards to help you understand intensities of some of them.

To keep track of your ratings, you'll need a score sheet (see Resources at the end of the book). These come in many shapes and sizes. Minimally, a sheet needs to list the characteristics under evaluation and provide a space for rating them. Most score sheets rate intensity using a numerical scale. For example, a "1" represents no intensity and a "10" represents the high end.

Some score sheets also list common descriptors. Generally, though, due to their subtlety, these descriptions are not rated on intensity but are merely noted as present/absent. All sheets have room to add descriptors which cuppers may detect on their own. Be innovative—often you can taste things in coffee that you would never expect to be there.

Identifying descriptors is one of the most challenging aspects of cupping. Part of the difficulty is actually knowing what you're tasting. Sometimes you taste things but don't recognize them as any flavor you've ever tried before. The inverse phenomenon is recognizing a taste that is so foreign to your expectation of a cup of coffee that you can't give the flavor its proper name.

→ HOW SHOULD YOU GRIND YOUR COFFEE?

Ideally, buy coffee as whole beans and grind it at home. This will help maintain its freshness. Ground coffee will stale much more quickly than whole beans. The appropriate grind size will depend on the method used for brewing. Generally, shorter extraction (brewing) times will require a smaller particle size. Don't be afraid to experiment, though. You may discover that slightly smaller or slightly larger than you're used to may work better for you and your brew method. Two basic types of grinder are available for home use.

BLADE GRINDERS These are relatively small and inexpensive. Their basic design is a closed chamber with a metal blade in the center. After the chamber is filled with coffee, the metal blade whirls at high speed to grind it. Particle size is determined by the length of time the grinder is run. Two problems arise because the coffee always remains in the chamber during grinding. First, acquiring an even, consistent particle size is nearly impossible because the coffee cannot escape the blade and is therefore constantly being ground finer (shaking the grinder up and down while grinding will help create a more even particle size). Second, the beans are subject to degradation due to the heat build-up in the chamber (try not to run the grinder for more than 10-second bursts).

BURR GRINDERS These are generally bigger and more expensive than blade grinders and while they can't produce perfectly uniform-sized grounds, they get much closer than blade grinders. Like spice mills, they work by passing the coffee through two metal burrs that are a set distance apart. The distance between the two burrs determines the particle size. Once the coffee is ground, it falls into a separate container, preventing the problems associated with blade grinders.

A QUALITY CUP

The delight and difficulty of coffee is that so many different things affect how it tastes. In fact, there are so many steps that the coffee must go through before it gets to your mouth that it's a wonder that we ever drink good coffee at all!

Quality, not surprisingly, begins with the plant. The plant's genetic makeup (species and variety) is one of the most important taste-determining factors. From there, maintaining a healthy plant is extremely important; a healthy tree is a tasty tree. Consequently, providing the plant with the proper nutrition, water and protection from pests and diseases is essential for high-quality production.

Elevation is often said to influence a coffee's taste greatly. Yet, while plants grown at

> "In our opinion, the best way to justify the price of anything (coffee or otherwise) is to focus on producing high-quality products. The customer should be able to taste the quality and appreciate the work that went into making it that way."
>
> —Joan Obra,
> Rusty's Hawaiian

different elevations do taste different, it's not because of the altitude, per se. Rather, it's the ambient temperatures found at each elevation. Temperature affects a bean's development, which translates into an assortment of flavors.

Temperature is relative to nearness to the equator, in that being closer produces hotter temperatures.

WHAT IS ESPRESSO?

Espresso is a method of brewing coffee. It is often defined as seven to nine grams of coffee packed under 30 to 40 pounds of pressure and extracted with one ounce of ~200°F water at nine bars of pressure for 20 to 30 seconds. However, as espresso culture has matured, manipulating these parameters has become acceptable.

Generally, the coffee used for espresso is a blend of three to seven origins, though single-origin espressos are regularly available. Coffees used for espresso were historically roasted darker to increase the body and decrease the acidity, which the high pressure of extraction can over-accentuate. These roast levels can still be found, though lighter roasts are the norm for many specialty coffee roasters.

However, higher elevations are cooler than lower ones. This is one reason why the same temperatures can be found at very different places on Earth. For example, Hawai'i is farther away from the equator than most other coffee-producing areas. Thus, our coffee regions are at lower elevations than in most other countries—sometimes practically at sea level!

The ripeness of cherries at harvest is very important. Ripe cherries are the safest bet for attaining the coffee's quality potential, but over-ripes can be quite tasty, too.

Out of the field, much of the processing impacts quality. Each cherry processing method imparts its own influence on the cup. Forced air-drying can taste different from sun drying. How long the coffee is aged before roasting will also play a role. These differences are neither good nor bad; they're just preferences.

Once the green coffee has left the farm, it is subject to the skill of the roaster. As already mentioned, roasting plays a major role in the organoleptic quality of the coffee. The roaster develops the flavor character; give the same coffee to 10 roasters and you'll get 10 different experiences. Once roasted, the coffee has a limited lifespan, and its quality will begin to decline.

Exposure to oxygen is a major culprit in the staling process. While exposure can be minimized, the coffee will also naturally degas, releasing compounds we'd enjoy drinking, not just smelling.

FROM TREE TO CUP: COFFEE BEGINS AS A GREEN FRUIT WHICH IS HAR-VESTED WHEN RIPE. THE SEED IS EXTRACTED, DRIED, PROCESSED AND FINALLY ROASTED.

ANDREW HETZEL

CONSULTANT

ANDREW HETZEL'S relationship with coffee has come a long way. As a teenager, he used it for "medicinal" purposes, just to keep him awake in school. Now it is the basis of his profession and a daily obsession. He's the owner of Coffee Strategies, a consulting company that assists coffee farmers and export associations to improve quality, marketplace competitiveness and profits.

Over the years, he's worked in coffee farming communities all over the world: in Africa, South America, Southeast Asia and even Yemen. At times, he's been a coffee specialist working on behalf of roasters and importers on the mainland, in Australia, China, Russia, South Korea, Switzerland, the UK and elsewhere. All that while, he's commuted from his home in Waimea, on the Big Island of Hawai'i. His combined flight mileage can circle the globe eight times each year.

Education is a fundamental aspect of his business. In his quest, he travels the globe teaching skills to coffee professionals, speaking at conferences and advising coffee exporters. The lessons he learns abroad are brought back home to benefit Hawai'i's farming community. He has also served as a board director (2013–2020)

for the 12,000-member Specialty Coffee Association, overseeing that group's Coffee Skills Program, the world's leading coffee trade education program.

With a practice focused on international development, largely funded by governments, aid organizations and NGO donors for disadvantaged farmers, not much of Andrew's work is seen in Hawai'i. "When I tell people that I work in coffee and live in Hawai'i, they ask to see my farm," says Hetzel. "It takes a little time to explain what I do, since this is a career path in Hawai'i agriculture that isn't in public view."

Nevertheless, he points out, there is a strong connection between Hawai'i and the international community working to make coffee sustainable for the future. "It's not at all unusual to be assisting coffee farmers in Myanmar or working with exporters in Brazil or elsewhere around the world and learn that one of them is from, has lived or studied in Hawai'i," says Hetzel. Hawai'i's footprint in the global agricultural community is much larger than one expects from the size of its population.

COFFEE STRATEGIES // www.coffeestrategies.com // 📷 : @cafemakers

COFFEE BREWING METHODS

In recent decades, there's been an explosion of coffee brewing devices to help us find the perfect cup. There's no perfect method or device, as each has its pros and cons. Brewing methods fall into three categories.

GRAVITY FED / PERCOLATION Water is poured over a bed of coffee and allowed to percolate through the grounds assisted only by gravity.

AUTOMATIC DRIP This is the typical plug-in coffeemaker most Americans are familiar with. The machine heats the water and, typically, sprays the coffee with water from above.

MANUAL DRIP The user manually pours hot water over the grounds. Your favorite café might call it "Chemex-brewed" or "pour-over" on the menu.

SINGLE-SERVE These electric, single-cup brewers use coffee pre-packaged in convenient pods. (Single-serve espresso machines, however, belong in the pressurized category.)

PERCOLATOR These cylindrical pots work on the automatic drip principle—hot water is sprayed over a bed of grounds and gravity pulls the water down. However, the brewing doesn't stop after the water is sprayed; rather, the brew is constantly cycled through the grounds until the machine is turned off.

NEAPOLITAN FLIP POT The water and coffee are placed in an inverted, spouted container over a heat source. Once the water reaches the proper temperature, the pot is flipped over and the water drips down through the grounds into an empty compartment.

FULL IMMERSION Coffee is fully immersed in water for a length of time before being filtered.

PRESS POT/FRENCH PRESS The coffee and hot water steep together for four to five minutes before a screen is gently pushed through the mixture to filter the coffee.

VACUUM POT This pot has two carafes aligned vertically. Water is placed in the bottom one, coffee in the top, a filter between. When heated, water is forced by steam to the top carafe, where the brewing occurs. After two to four minutes, the heat is removed, water vapor in the lower carafe condenses and the resulting vacuum sucks the brewed coffee down from the top carafe, leaving the grounds behind.

COLD BREW Typically, a greater coffee/water ratio is used in this method. Cold water steeps the coffee for an extended period of time, usually about 24 hours, in a refrigerator. The resultant brew, after filtering, is more concentrated than most other brew methods.

"COWBOY" COFFEE This is cupping without the spoons. Water is poured over grounds and drunk, unfiltered.

MEDITERRANEAN/TURKISH/GREEK STYLE Finely ground coffee is boiled in a pot along with sugar and spices (typically cardamom).

PRESSURIZED Water under greater-than-atmospheric pressure is forced through a bed of coffee, typically producing a more concentrated brew than other methods.

ESPRESSO Highly pressurized water is forced through a puck of finely ground coffee to create a very concentrated brew. See page 57.

MOKA POT This is also known as stovetop espresso, though it isn't espresso at all. Water is boiled through coffee in a middle compartment from a lower compartment. The brew ends up in an upper compartment whence the coffee can be easily poured.

AEROPRESS This is a plunger pot/espresso hybrid. After the water and coffee brew together, a plunger is used to force the brew through a filter. The pressure is more than that of a plunger pot but less than that of an espresso machine.

HOW SHOULD YOU STORE YOUR COFFEE?

Quite simply, don't. The best coffees are the freshest ones. Buy only enough coffee to last two to three weeks. Keep it in an airtight container in a cool, dark place.

If you absolutely must store coffee for longer than three weeks, keep it in an airtight container and store it in the freezer. Minimize how many times you bring it out. Temperature changes and condensation will likely work against you.

The age at which a roasted coffee is no longer desirable depends, of course, on the drinker. Discerning drinkers can begin to notice staling in one or two weeks. However, most drinkers probably won't notice it for four to six weeks.

The final factor affecting the cup quality is how the coffee is brewed. No method is better than another; they each offer something worthwhile and each has its own influence on the final taste. Brew methods fall into three categories. See "Coffee Brewing Methods" on pages 60–61 for more information.

....

"It's funny how with all the fancy coffee shit around, a simple French press and a few cents worth of beans make a little coffee nirvana."

—Laura Sielen Sobjack, coffee aficionado

....

The dizzying variety of coffee brewers exist because there are so many factors that can be manipulated in the brewing process to influence the final outcome:

* particle size of the grounds
* water temperature
* water quality
* water pressure during extraction
* agitation of the brew slurry
* strength of the brew (the coffee/water ratio)
* materials the containers are made from (plastic, metal, glass, etc.)
* shape and design of the brew basket
* contact time between the coffee and water
* type of filter

The continuous invention of gadgets and gizmos that serve, brew, store and celebrate coffee in the home suggests that people experience coffee on an intimate, personal level. Coffee is not just something we mindlessly quaff but, like wine, something that affects us viscerally and intellectually.

Coffee means something to us and says something about us. The increased demand for specific roast levels, origins and ethical coffees demonstrates an awareness of our senses. Coffee is no longer just coffee. Instead, it is a part of our social and individual identity.

The infusion of coffee into our mental framework is best exemplified by the modern barista. "Barista" is the Italian word for a bartender in an Italian-style bar. However, in English, a barista is the person making and serving the coffee, typically in a coffeehouse. Some baristas take their craft very seriously. Like athletes, they devote immeasurable hours to improving their skills. They cup voraciously, pull countless shots of espresso and texturize copious amounts of milk. Some join the Barista Guild and participate in prestigious competitions.

Coffee competitions began after the turn of the 21st century and have become immensely popular. They are the venue for showcasing talent and passion for coffee. They began with the Barista Championship, a competition that focused on espresso-based drinks. Competitors were asked to make several different beverages and were graded not only on the organoleptic quality and presentation of the beverages but also on technical skills, professionalism and cleanliness. In the last decade, many other coffee competitions were developed, all of which culminate in a world championship competition: Coffee in Good Spirits, Latte Art, Cup Tasters, Brewers Cup, Cezve/Ibrik, and Aeropress. Perfectly in line with barista-focused competitions, competitions focused on roasting also exist (see Chapter Seven).

Coffee has become entwined with our collective psyche. It will continue to imbue our lives in unpredictable ways. Those of us with a passion for coffee hope that this ethereal beverage will influence our culture forevermore.

CHAPTER 5

COOKING WITH COFFEE

SAVORIES, SWEETS & BEVERAGES

IN THIS CHAPTER, you can drink your coffee and eat it, too!

Coffee makes an excellent ingredient in an array of dishes. Think of it as a spice like pepper or vanilla. Whether you use it brewed or ground, coffee's complexity and depth offer new avenues for many different foods. Different varieties, cherry processes and roast levels each offer a slightly different final dish. The combinations are endless!

Here, you'll find 20 coffee-inspired recipes created by prestigious chefs and everyday folk from across the Islands. Among them are savory en-trées, tantalizing desserts and thirst-quenching drinks.

When cooking with coffee, using high-quality, freshly roasted Hawai'i coffee is best. While some of this chapter's recipes call for a specific brand or variety, you can always substitute it with your favorite Island coffee.

Open up your kitchen to some creative cooking and discover why coffee doesn't have to be confined to your cup anymore!

....

"Now you're getting warmer;
coffee with the latter,
coffee with the former;
coffee with the steak,
coffee with the soup,
coffee with the clams
in a chilly group;
yes, and with a cocktail
I could do,
so bring me coffee
with the cocktail, too."

—Ogden Nash,
from "Coffee With the Meal"

....

KONA COFFEE-MARINATED EGGPLANT

YEHUDA AND AVIVA PLAUT

This marinated eggplant recipe is a past winner of the annual Kona Coffee Cultural Festival recipe contest.

3 medium	Italian eggplant
	Salt
	Olive oil
½ cup	Kona coffee
½ cup	balsamic vinegar
1 T.	honey
10 cloves	garlic, crushed and minced
1	sweet red pepper, roasted and sliced thinly

Peel the eggplant, slice into ½-inch thick rounds and sprinkle with salt. Brush olive oil on each side and cook on a hot cast-iron pan or griddle until soft, turning once or twice. When you push down with a fork, it should be completely soft. The eggplant will look a bit blackened.

Combine the coffee, balsamic vinegar and honey and cook, reducing to half the volume. The texture should be a little thinner than syrup.

Layer the eggplant with pepper and garlic as it comes off the hot pan, drizzling the reduced coffee-vinegar liberally on each layer. Store in the refrigerator in a container with a tight lid. This becomes tastier over time, so you should make this a day or two in advance. Serve on Kona Coffee Pumpernickel Bread (see recipe, page 95).

COFFEE POKE

ASH DANAO, FOUR SEASONS RESORT HUALĀLAI

1 lb.	'ahi, small diced
1 T.	'inamona (roasted kukui nuts)
1 cup	red onion, brunoise
½ cup	ogo (seaweed)
¼ cup	chives, thinly cut on the bias
½ cup	hearts of palm, fine julienne
	'alaea (red Hawaiian sea salt), to taste
½ cup	avocado, small diced
1 T.	olive oil

Sauce

1 cup	double-steeped Kona coffee (see Chef's Tip)
2 T.	honey
1 tsp.	dried Hawaiian chili pepper, ground
¼ tsp.	'alaea
½ cup	cornstarch slurry (equal parts water & cornstarch)

Make the sauce a day ahead of time to give the sauce time to bloom to full flavor. Combine sauce ingredients, except for the cornstarch slurry, in a pot. Bring to a boil over high heat, but don't reduce or your sauce will be bitter. When the sauce comes to a boil, whisk in slurry to thicken until the sauce coats the back of a spoon. (You may not need all the slurry.) Set aside to cool completely. Store in an airtight container.

Combine the fish, 'inamona, ogo, chives, hearts of palm and red onion in a large mixing bowl. Mix together thoroughly, then add the sauce ¼ cup at a time. Add avocado and olive oil and continue to mix, taste and add sauce to preference.

Serves 5

CHEF'S TIP: To make double-steeped coffee, brew coffee as usual, strain, then re-brew the strained liquid.

KONA COFFEE PANIOLO BAKED BEANS

MARTIN RATHBUN, MARTY CAKES & COMPANY
This dish makes a perfect side pairing with Coffee-Barbecue Pulled Pork (see page 83).

4 strips	bacon, cut to ¾-inch pieces
1 lb.	mixed vegetables, cut stir-fry style (see Chef's Tip)
1 T.	Coffee Rub (see recipe, page 79)
1 cup	brewed Kona coffee
1 cup	Barbecue Sauce (see recipe, page 83)
½ cup	brown sugar, firmly packed
1 T.	shoyu (soy sauce)
1 can (16-oz.)	chili beans in mild sauce
1 can (15.5-oz.)	kidney beans, rinsed and drained
1 can (15.5-oz.)	cannellini beans, rinsed and drained
1 can (15.5-oz.)	black beans, rinsed and drained

Preheat oven to 375°F. Heat the bacon in a skillet over medium heat until almost crisp. Drain all but about 1 teaspoon of the bacon drippings. Add cut vegetables, 1 tablespoon of Coffee Rub seasoning and fry until tender, about 5 minutes stirring occasionally.

Mix the brewed coffee, Barbecue Sauce, brown sugar and shoyu in a large bowl. Stir in all of the beans and the bacon-vegetable mixture.

Spoon into a 3- to 4-quart casserole dish, coated with non-stick cooking spray. Cover and bake in the preheated oven for 30 minutes. Uncover, stir and bake uncovered for an additional 15 minutes or until hot and bubbly.

Yields about 10 cups

CHEF'S TIP: Frozen stir-fry vegetables are an excellent alternative to slicing your own!

COCONUT PORTER &
MAUI COFFEE SMOKED BRISKET

LYNDON HONDA, SHERATON MAUI RESORT & SPA

This brisket, infused with the flavors of Maui Brewing's Coconut Porter and MauiGrown Coffee's Mokka Peaberry, takes some advance preparation, but the payoff is worth the wait.

3 to 4 lb.	beef brisket
1 can	Maui Brewing Company Coconut Porter beer
¼ cup	MauiGrown Coffee Mokka Peaberry, medium roast, finely ground
¼ cup	kosher salt
¼ cup	brown sugar
2 T.	paprika
2 T.	ancho chili powder
2 T.	black pepper, ground
2 T.	onion powder
2 T.	garlic powder
	Wood chips for smoking
	Coffee–Coconut Porter Mop Sauce (see opposite page)

Soak brisket in Coconut Porter beer for 2 days. Drain and reserve 1 cup beer for Mop Sauce and the remainder for soaking wood chips. Combine remaining ingredients for dry rub. Pat brisket dry, rub with seasoning and let stand for 2 hours. While brisket stands, soak wood chips for at least 30 minutes in reserved beer. Smoke brisket at 220 to 230°F for about 4 to 6 hours, applying Coffee–Coconut Porter Mop Sauce liberally every hour.

CHEF'S TIP: Using finely ground coffee creates a more intense flavor.

COFFEE–COCONUT PORTER
MOP SAUCE

1 cup	Maui Brewing Company Coconut Porter (reserved from brisket soak)
½ cup	MauiGrown Coffee Mokka Peaberry, medium roast
½ cup	beef broth
¼ cup	Worcestershire sauce
	Cornstarch slurry (equal parts water and cornstarch, whisked together)

Combine ingredients through Worcestershire sauce in a sauce pot and bring to a boil. Whisk in cornstarch slurry to thicken to desired consistency and simmer for 20 to 30 minutes.

COFFEE-RUBBED FILET MIGNON WITH MOCHA–CHILE SAUCE

GENO SARMIENTO, NICK'S FISHMARKET MAUI
Molokaʻi coffee is a full-bodied and high-quality coffee that complements the filet mignon in this recipe.

1 whole	beef tenderloin, trimmed
2 sprigs	fresh thyme
2 cups	molasses
2 cups	brewed Molokaʻi Estate Midnight's Roast
¼ cup	ground coffee beans (use same coffee as above)
	Hawaiian salt
	Ground black pepper

Mix brewed coffee and molasses together, add thyme. Rub the coffee grounds, salt and pepper on whole tenderloin. Marinate the beef in the coffee–molasses mix for at least 4 hours. Cut and portion beef to desired weight and grill. Serve with Mocha–Chile Sauce (recipe opposite) and Chimmichuri (recipe below).

CHIMICHURRI

Use fresh herbs for this recipe, not dried.

½ cup	cilantro		½ cup	red wine vinegar
½ cup	basil		2 pieces	Hawaiian chili pepper
2 T.	thyme		1 clove	garlic
½ cup	Italian parsley		¾ cup	olive oil
2 T.	oregano			Salt and pepper (to taste)

Blend all ingredients, adding in oil slowly, until smooth.

MOCHA–CHILE SAUCE

2 T.	olive oil
2 T.	unsalted butter
2 T.	roasted garlic, pureed
1	large onion, diced
1¼ cup	ancho chile, chopped
4 T.	tomato paste
1 cup	brewed Moloka'i Estate Midnight's Roast
1 whole	roasted red pepper, chopped
1 cup	chicken stock
2 T.	chili powder
½ cup	bittersweet chocolate
1 cup	veal demi-glace
2 oz.	cold butter, diced

Heat oil and butter in a saucepan. Add onion, garlic and ancho chile, and cook until soft. Add tomato paste and toast for 1 minute. Add coffee, simmer for 3 minutes. Add red pepper, chicken stock, chili powder and chocolate, simmer until slightly thick, about 30 to 45 minutes. Transfer to a blender and blend until smooth. Add in the demi-glace and butter, mix well and season to taste.

BRAISED OSSO BUCO WITH COFFEE MOLE

ASH DANAO, FOUR SEASONS RESORT HUALĀLAI

3 lbs.	beef shank, 3-inch cut
1 cup	peanut or soybean oil
½ T.	cracked black pepper
1 T.	kosher or sea salt
½ lb.	onion
¼ lb.	celery
¼ lb.	carrots
1 cup	plum sake
1 cup	garlic, minced
4 cups	beef stock

Tie into a cheesecloth sachet:

¼ oz.	fresh thyme, leaves only
¼ oz.	fresh rosemary, leaves only

Prepare a hot pan with oil to brown the osso bucco. Season each piece of beef with salt and pepper. Working in batches, brown the meat all around, then transfer to a large roasting pan. In the same pan used to cook the beef, caramelize the onion, celery and carrots. Be sure the pan is very hot.

Add caramelized vegetables and herb sachet to the roasting pan with the beef. Deglaze the cooking pan with plum sake and reduce by half. Once reduced, add to the roasting pan with beef stock and garlic.

Cover the pan tightly with foil and bake in a 375°F oven for 5 hours.

Pull out and check doneness. If beef is tender, remove and cool; if not, replace into the oven for up to an additional hour until soft.

Serve with Coffee Mole (see following page).

Serves 4

COFFEE MOLE

¼ cup	Hawaiian chili, dried
3	Hāmākua vine-ripened tomatoes
1 cup	olive oil
1 cup	shallots
1 cup	garlic, peeled
2 tsp.	ground cumin
1 tsp.	dried thyme
2 tsp.	ground cinnamon
1 T.	ground allspice
1 T.	sugar
2 tsp.	kosher or sea salt
3 cups	cold-brewed, dark-roast Hawaiian coffee
½ cup	tomato paste
¼ lb.	dark chocolate, chopped
2 cups	water

Preheat oven to 400°F. Combine all ingredients except chocolate and water in a large bowl and mix to coat vegetables well with seasonings. Transfer to roasting pan and spread evenly. Roast until caramelized but not burnt.

Add roasted vegetables and water to blender and blend until smooth. On the last blend, add chocolate and blend until sauce is uniformly smooth. Allow to cool before storing or use immediately as a sauce.

Makes about 1 quart

COFFEE-RUBBED GRILLED PORK CHOPS

MARTIN RATHBUN, MARTY CAKES & COMPANY

The Coffee Rub seasoning mix in this recipe is excellent on all types of grilled meats—beef, lamb, veal, pork and poultry.

1 cup	Coffee Rub (recipe follows)
4 to 6	pork chops, center-cut, bone-in
	Olive oil

Select pork chops that are at least 1 to 2 inches thick. Rub the chops well with Coffee Rub and place in a zip-top bag. Allow to rest for a minimum of 5 minutes to an hour.

Brush the meat with olive oil and grill over high heat for 4 to 5 minutes per side, or until an internal temperature of 145°F is reached.

Remove from grill and allow to rest, covered, 5 to 10 minutes before serving

Makes 4 to 6 pork chops

COFFEE RUB SEASONING MIX

½ cup	brown sugar, firmly packed		¼ cup	garlic powder
			¼ cup	paprika
½ cup	espresso powder		¼ cup	salt
¼ cup	dry mustard		2 T.	ground black pepper

Combine all ingredients in a large bowl and mix well. This mixture will remain fresh for several weeks when stored in an airtight container. To use, rub the seasoning onto the meat and allow the meat to rest for 30 to 60 minutes. Brush the meat with oil and grill to desired doneness.

Yields a generous 2 cups

PORK CHOPS & RED EYE GRAVY

MARK "GOOCH" NOGUCHI, PILI GROUP

I know everyone gets excited about double-cut pork chops, but I'm a fan of thin-cut chops, cooked quickly in a ripping hot pan or over a blazing hot grill.

8	¼-inch thin-cut, bone-in pork chops
	Oil or lard, for cooking

Brine

2 qts.	water		1 T.	whole coffee beans, cracked
2 pieces	bay leaf			
2 sprigs	rosemary		4 T.	salt
1 T.	shoyu		2 T.	sugar
			2 T.	black peppercorn

Combine brine ingredients, bring up to a boil, cool and reserve. Brine chops overnight, but not longer than 24 hours. The brine can start to overpower the pork in flavor.

Take your chops out, pat dry, season with salt and pepper. Get a cast-iron pan ripping hot and add enough oil to evenly coat the pan. If you really wanna level up your pork game, use lard. You know your pan is ready when the oil is shimmering across the pan, and it starts to release wisps of white smoke. If you've got billowing clouds, you went too far. Put the fire out and order take out. But if you're ready to go, add your chops—don't crowd the pan, good food takes time.

Cook pork in small batches to the temperature that you like. If you know where your pork comes from, and you trust your farmers like I do, you don't have to cook the chop to death. When all your chops are finished, reserve in a low-heat oven on paper towel. Don't throw away the fat in the pan—you'll need it for the gravy.

When the gravy's done, Take those chops out, put 'em on a plate, serve that gravy on the side. And beer... Don't forget to drink beer...

Serves 4 to 6

CHEF'S TIP: Brine can be made up to a week ahead. If making it day-of, cut water to 1 quart, bring to a boil, then add 1½ quarts of ice to chill it.

RED EYE GRAVY

½	small onion, diced		2 T.	flat-leaf Italian parsley, chopped
2 T.	unsalted butter, cut into ½-inch cubes		1 T.	oregano, chopped
3 T.	all-purpose flour		½	lemon, juiced
½ cup	brewed coffee			Salt
¼ cup	water			Fresh cracked pepper

   Reduce pan to medium heat. Add onions first, cooking until translucent. Now add butter, then flour; with a wooden spoon, stir to evenly homogenize the flour into the fat—you're making a roux. When all flour lumps have been worked out, add coffee and water slowly, whisking to prevent lumps. Now turn the fire down so the gravy barely simmers, cook for 8 to 10 minutes or until it doesn't feel grainy in the mouth. Add chopped fresh herbs, lemon juice, salt and pepper.

COFFEE-BARBECUE PULLED PORK

MARTIN RATHBUN, MARTY CAKES & COMPANY

2 T.	oil, divided		3 cups	Coffee Barbecue Sauce (recipe follows)
1 cup	chopped onion		5 lbs.	pork butt roast
1 cup	chopped green pepper			Salt and pepper
1 cup	strong brewed coffee (see Chef's Tip, page 97)			Split sandwich buns

In a medium sauté pan, sauté onion and green pepper in 1 tablespoon oil until softened. Add the coffee and 1 cup of Barbecue Sauce. Simmer for several minutes.

Heat remaining tablespoon of oil in a roasting pan or Dutch oven to medium-high heat. Sear the roast on all sides, about 10 minutes total. Add vegetable mixture over roast and cook 2 to 4 hours in the oven until the meat is tender enough to shred with a fork.

Remove roast from the pan and shred meat using two forks. Strain the pan juices and mix 1 cup of pan juices with remaining 2 cups of Barbecue Sauce. Add to the shredded meat to desired moistness. Season with salt and pepper. Serve on warmed sandwich buns with remaining Barbecue Sauce on the side.

Yields about 10 cups (enough for 12 to 15 sandwiches)

COFFEE BARBECUE SAUCE

4 cups	ketchup		1 T.	onion powder
2 cups	black coffee		1 T.	ground mustard
1 cup	apple cider vinegar		2 T.	lemon juice
1 cup	brown sugar		2 T.	Worcestershire sauce
1 cup	granulated sugar		2 T.	liquid hickory smoke
1 T.	cracked black pepper			

Place all ingredients in a large saucepan and stir to combine. Bring to a boil and cook for several minutes, stirring occasionally. Reduce to a simmer and cook, uncovered, stirring frequently for 1 to 1½ hours. Cool and refrigerate, covered, until needed.

Makes about 5 cups

ALTERNATE SLOW COOKER METHOD: Prepare vegetable mixture and sear roast as described above. Place roast in a slow cooker. Pour Barbecue Sauce–vegetable mixture over roast. Cook on high for 5 to 6 hours, or on low for 8 hours, until the meat is fork tender. Complete recipe as directed above.

SAVORY / PORK

COFFEE JERK CHICKEN

ASH DANAO, FOUR SEASONS RESORT HUALĀLAI

1 T.	garlic powder		1 tsp.	paprika
1 T.	dried Hawaiian chili, ground		1 tsp.	ground all spice
2 tsp.	onion powder		1 tsp.	ground black pepper
2 tsp.	dried thyme		1 tsp.	ground nutmeg
2 tsp.	dried parsley		½ tsp.	ground cinnamon
1 tsp.	sugar		1 cup	medium-roast coffee, finely ground
1 T.	brown sugar		4 lbs.	chicken breast
2 tsp.	salt			

Combine all ingredients except for chicken.

Coat chicken with seasoning mix thoroughly on one side. Heat oven to 400°F. Preheat a pan over medium-high heat, with oil to cover the bottom.

Place the chicken in the hot pan, coated-side down, to sear and caramelize, about 1 minute. Turn the chicken over. Put the pan in the oven to finish cooking, until internal temperature reaches 155°F.

Pull out and let the chicken rest for 3 minutes before serving.

Serves 8

CHEF'S TIP: You can make this seasoning mix in advance; it will keep for three months in an airtight container.

COFFEE CARAMEL
CRÈME BRÛLÉE

MARTIN RATHBUN, MARTY CAKES & COMPANY

4 oz.	coffee beans		2½ cups	heavy cream
2½ cups	half & half		10	egg yolks
10 oz.	sugar, divided		½ tsp.	salt
⅔ cup	water		6 to 8 T.	coarse sugar

Place the coffee beans in a plastic or paper bag and wrap in a kitchen towel. Rough-crack the beans by hitting with a mallet or rolling pin. Empty the cracked beans into a sauce pan and add the half & half. Bring to a boil, remove from heat, cover and allow to steep for 20 minutes to an hour.

Preheat the oven to 325°F. Stir 5 ounces of the sugar with the ⅔ cup of water in a saucepan over low heat until the sugar dissolves into a syrup. Increase the heat to medium-high and bring to a boil, brushing down the sides of the pan with a wet pastry brush to prevent sugar crystals from forming. Continue to boil without stirring, swirling the pan occasionally, until the syrup is a deep amber color—about 5 minutes.

In the meantime, in a separate saucepan, heat the 2½ cups of cream until just ready to boil. Remove the syrup from the heat and add in the hot cream while stirring briskly. Take care as the mixture will bubble up while the cream is added. Return the resulting caramel to the stove on low heat and stir until it is smooth and free of lumps. Strain the coffee-infused half & half into the caramel and discard the coffee beans.

RECIPE CONTINUES ›››››

Whisk the egg yolks, salt and remaining 5 ounces of sugar in a large bowl to blend. Gradually whisk in the cream mixture. Strain the custard mixture into a large measuring cup and portion onto 6-ounce ramekins set in a shallow pan of water. Bake in the preheated oven until the custard is just set, about 10 to 15 minutes. The custards should jiggle slightly when moved. Remove the custards from the water bath, allow them to cool slightly and then refrigerate until cold.

To serve, add 1 tablespoon of coarse sugar to the top of each custard and shake gently to disperse it and even it out. Melt the sugar with a small torch or place under the oven broiler for a few minutes, until the sugar is melted, and the desired browned color is reached.

Makes 6 to 8 servings

SWEETS & BAKED GOODS

COFFEE SHORTBREAD

ABIGAIL LANGLAS, CAKE WORKS BAKERY

1 lb. plus 2 oz.	unsalted butter, softened
10 oz.	powdered sugar
5 oz.	vanilla extract
3 T.	medium-ground coffee grounds
1 tsp.	salt
1 lb. plus 3 oz.	pastry flour

Cream together butter and sugar. Mix in vanilla, coffee and salt. Add pastry flour and mix until just combined. Portion out into 1½-inch balls, using a 1-ounce scoop, and bake at 300°F for 15 minutes. Shortbread is done when it is still pale (it shouldn't be browned) and is springy when touched.

Makes 60 pieces

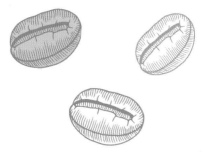

COFFEE ANGLAISE AND DOUGHNUTS

LEE ANNE WONG, CHEF-OWNER, KOKO HEAD CAFÉ
This Coffee Anglaise is good for all things sweet, and can be served as a dipping sauce, dressed sauce or turned into ice cream. At Koko Head Café we serve it with doughnuts.

2 cups plus 1½ T.	whole milk
2 cups plus 1½ T.	heavy cream
¼ cup	finely ground coffee
1 tsp.	vanilla extract
8 large	egg yolks
1 cup	granulated sugar

In a heavy-bottomed saucepan, simmer the milk, cream, coffee grounds and vanilla for approximately 10 minutes to infuse the coffee. Do not let the mixture boil.

Whisk the eggs and sugar in a clean bowl until it is pale yellow and ribbons form when lifting the whisk.

Add a cup of the hot cream mixture into the beaten egg yolks and sugar, whisking to incorporate, tempering your egg yolks.

Add the egg mixture to the pot with the remaining cream and cook on medium heat while stirring continuously until the anglaise is thickened and coats the back of a spoon. Transfer the anglaise to an ice bath to cool down immediately. Serve chilled.

SESAME DOUGHNUTS

1 cup	sugar		1 tsp.	salt
2 large	eggs		½ tsp.	baking soda
1 cup	sour cream		1 tsp.	baking powder
½ tsp.	vanilla extract		2 T.	black sesame seeds
⅓ cup	melted butter			powdered or cinnamon sugar
3½ cups	cake flour			

Beat eggs and sugar in a stand mixer on medium speed with paddle to ribbon stage (pale and thick). Add the sour cream and vanilla and mix until incorporated. Scrape down the sides of the bowl.

Slowly pour in the melted butter. Turn speed down to low and add the dry ingredients, including sesame seeds. Mix until just incorporated, being careful not to overwork the dough. Scrape down the bowls to make sure everything is mixed.

Line a half-sheet tray with parchment paper. Spread doughnut dough out and top with another piece of parchment. Chill in the refrigerator until the dough is firm.

Preheat fry oil to 350°F. Roll dough into 1½-inch diameter balls. Fry a few pieces at a time until golden and not raw in the middle, being sure not to crowd the oil. Coat in a light dusting of powdered sugar or cinnamon sugar.

Makes about 50 to 55 pieces

FLOURLESS CHOCOLATE CAKE

MARTIN RATHBUN, MARTY CAKES & COMPANY

Jam of any flavor—raspberry, apricot, cherry—works very well for this. Or try an Island-inspired flavor like liliko'i butter or mango preserves.

1½ cups	semisweet chocolate
½ cup	butter (1 stick)
1 cup	granulated sugar
4 large	eggs at room temperature, separated
1 tsp.	Coffee Reduction Syrup, warmed but not hot (see recipe, pg. 97)
½ cup	warmed fruit preserves

Whipped Cream

1 cup	cold heavy cream
½ tsp.	vanilla extract
2 T.	powdered sugar

Prepare whipped cream by beating the cream and vanilla in the bowl of a mixer on medium-high speed, until soft peaks form. Add the powdered sugar and continue to beat until stiff. Keep chilled until ready to serve.

Preheat oven to 350°F. Grease an 8-inch springform cake pan with butter or non-stick cooking spray and line with parchment.

Melt the chocolate and butter in a medium saucepan, stirring frequently, until melted and smooth. Stir in the sugar. Whisk in the egg yolks, one at a time, mixing thoroughly between each addition. Stir in warm coffee syrup and set aside.

Beat the egg whites in the bowl of a mixer on high speed until almost stiff. Gradually fold in the chocolate mixture in three additions, until no whites are visible. Spread into the prepared cake pan and bake in preheated oven for 25 to 30 minutes, or until the edges are puffed and firm. Cool on a wire rack for 30 minutes, then cover and chill.

To serve:

Remove the sides of the springform pan and place cake on a serving dish. Place fruit preserves in a small saucepan and warm slightly. Stir and spread the preserve over the cake. Garnish with whipped cream.

Makes one 8-inch cake

COFFEE SOURDOUGH

SHANNON WIENER, FIRE DANCE PIZZA
A coffee-infused recipe for those with bread-baking experience.

Baker Percentages:

100%	bread flour
20%	active liquid starter
80%	hydration water or coffee
2%	salt
2%	instant coffee granules (if not using coffee as liquid)

Coffee Sourdough Formula:

900 g	bread flour
200 g	active liquid starter
700 g	coffee or water*
20 g	salt

*Add 20 g instant coffee if using water instead of brewed coffee

Mix:

Mix flour, starter and all but 50 grams of water until all the flour is hydrated and the ingredients incorporated.

Autolyse:

Leave untouched for 20 minutes to 1 hour.

Add salt:

Add salt to 50 grams of water to make a slurry, then mix into dough gently until most of the water has been soaked up. Don't be too forceful because the water will eventually be fully incorporated during the rest of the bulk fermentation.

Makes 2 loaves

KONA COFFEE PUMPERNICKEL BREAD

YEHUDA AND AVIVA PLAUT

1 cup	strong Kona coffee (at 110°F)
¼ cup	milk
1 T.	vegetable oil
1 ½ T.	molasses
½ cup	whole wheat flour
1 ½ to 2 cups	unbleached all-purpose flour
1 cup	rye flour
1 tsp.	salt
2 T.	unsweetened cocoa powder
1 T.	caraway seed
1 ½ tsp.	active dry yeast

Mix warm coffee, yeast and molasses and proof the yeast (5 minutes). Add salt, cocoa powder, caraway seeds, rye and whole wheat flours. Stir vigorously for 3 to 5 minutes to develop the gluten. Add unbleached all-purpose flour ½ cup at a time, stirring, keeping dough moist and a bit sticky.

When unable to stir any more, turn onto a floured board and knead for 5 minutes, flouring hands as needed. Make a neat ball, oil the surface and let rise in a covered bowl for 1 to 1½ hours.

After rising, knead dough for 1 to 2 minutes. Divide dough in half; form into loaves. Let rise for 45 minutes.

Bake at 350°F for 35 to 40 minutes. Remove from oven and let cool before slicing.

Makes 2 loaves

AFFOGATO

MARTIN RATHBUN, MARTY CAKES & COMPANY
An affogato, Italian for "drowned," is an Italian coffee-based dessert. While the recipe of the affogato is more or less standard in Italy, consisting of a scoop of vanilla gelato topped ("drowned") with a shot of espresso, variations exist—try adding a shot of liqueur, a sprinkling of nuts, coconut or berries, or changing the ice cream flavor.

This simplicity of this dessert is made luxurious by using the finest ice cream or gelato and espresso.

1 scoop	ice cream or gelato
2 oz.	espresso
1 T.	Coffee Reduction Syrup (recipe follows)

Place ice cream or gelato in a dessert glass or compote and pour over the espresso. Finish with a drizzle of Coffee Syrup.

Serves 1

COFFEE REDUCTION SYRUP

1 cup	sugar
1 cup	strong brewed coffee

Combine the sugar and coffee in a small saucepan. Bring to a boil, stirring occasionally. Reduce heat and simmer until the mixture reduces to 1 cup.

Cool to room temperature and transfer to a covered container. Store in the refrigerator for up to 1 month.

CHEF'S TIP: For strong brewed coffee, stir ½ cup of medium-grind coffee into 3¾ cups 205°F water in a saucepan. Allow to stand to cool, then strain.

ESPRESSO MARTINI

SONI POMASKI, MOON & TURTLE

1 shot	espresso
1½ oz.	Stolichnaya vanilla vodka
1 oz.	Frangelico
½ oz.	simple syrup

Fill a shaker with ice and begin pulling a shot of espresso. While your shot is running, add vodka, Frangelico and simple syrup to the shaker. Drop your shot into the shaker as soon as it's done. Shake vigorously, at least 20 times, and strain into a chilled martini glass. Serve immediately.

Serves 1

THE QUINNTESSENTIAL

QUINN MEARS, FORMERLY OF ENCORE SALOON

Author's Note: This drink, created by Quinn Mears while he was bar manager at Encore Saloon, makes use of nitro cold brew. Cold brew is, as you may have guessed, brewed with cool or room temp water, typically overnight. The long brew yields a concentrated coffee, which is often diluted. To give cold brew a creamy texture and to have it easily and immediately available, it is infused with nitrogen gas and connected to a bar tap. When poured, it has the same visual cascade of bubbles as Guinness beer.

1½ oz.	mezcal
½ oz.	demerara simple syrup
½ oz.	Cynar
	Splash of Fernet
2 oz.	nitro cold brew

Combine ingredients in a shaker with ice. Shake vigorously, double-strain into a coupe glass. Garnish with fresh grated nutmeg over top.

Serves 1

KAUA'I COFFEE SHAVE ICE & COCKTAIL MIXER SYRUP

GIDA SNYDER, GIDA'S KITCHEN PANTRY

I like to use Moloa'a Bay Estate Roast for this syrup. It's grown, handpicked and small-batch processed on our beautiful island of Kaua'i. The medium roast with bright citrus and floral notes makes a versatile and refreshing syrup.

4 cups	water		1½ tsp.	citric acid
4 cups	organic sugar			(optional, if you'd like to can and
4 oz.	finely ground Moloa'a Bay Estate Roast coffee			preserve it; otherwise, it will last about 10 days in your refrigerator)

Bring water to a boil. Turn off heat and dissolve sugar, then add coffee. Stir and let steep for 10 to 30 minutes. Strain once through a sieve to remove largest particles, then again through a coffee filter. Store in glass container.

Makes 6 cups

SHAVE ICE (PICTURED)

Pour Cockatil Mixer Syrup over shaved ice. Top with sweetened condensed milk or coconut milk.

KAUA'I COFFEE FRAPPÉ

Combine in high-powered blender, pour into chilled glass.

1 cup	ice		1 shot	espresso
2 oz.	Coffee Syrup		1 shot	vodka (optional)

KAUA'I COFFEE SODA

2 oz.	Coffee Syrup		Cream or half & half
12 oz.	sparkling water		(optional)

Pour syrup and sparkling water over ice and stir. Top with cream or milk. For a Vietnamese-style Coffee Soda, use sweetened condensed milk and add a shot of espresso.

CHEF'S TIP: To can, add citric acid to the mixture and follow water bath canning directions for glass canning jars. Syrup will last up to a year unopened.

SACKS OF GREEN COFFEE AT WAIALUA ESTATE COFFEE,
NORTH SHORE, OʻAHU

CHAPTER 6

COFFEE SCIENCE AND ETHICS

SUSTAINABILITY, ECONOMICS & SOCIAL AWARENESS

A BOOK ABOUT COFFEE in the Islands would be remiss to not mention anything about the role of science, because Hawai'i is one of the few coffee-growing locales that has the resources and talent to study coffee from seed to cup. Not a single area of coffee production is inaccessible to Hawai'i's scientists. Most of the scientific research in Hawai'i has been conducted directly to benefit the state's local farmers and industry. Since 1898, the University of Hawai'i College of Tropical Agriculture and Human Resources (CTAHR) has conducted most of the coffee science research in the state, although the Hawai'i Agriculture Research Center (HARC) has also contributed important research in coffee genomics, tissue culture and molecular biology for more than 30 years. More recently, the attention grabber has been HARC's intensive breeding program. Not only have HARC scientists been breeding for disease resistance, but they have created singular Hawai'i varieties with unique flavor profiles and desirable horticultural traits. In recent years, the US Pacific Basin Agricultural Research Center (PBARC) has begun work on coffee. Without the work of scientists, Hawai'i coffee would not be the high-quality, viable crop that it is today.

TREES SPRAYED WITH KAOLIN IN AN EXPERIMENT TO TEST THE EFFECT ON THE PLANT'S PHYSIOLOGY AND ITS ABILITY TO COMBAT THE COFFEE BERRY BORER

In the past, coffee science in Hawai'i was geared toward helping farmers with production and engineering support, though there has been sporadic work on big-picture topics like origin identification and cup quality. Occasionally, industry analyses and marketing reports were made to help farmers and roasters better understand consumer preferences and industry trends. Today, research goals tend to focus on the immediate needs of farmers, such as pest control and synchronization of flowering.

This year, PBARC began creating a coffee germplasm collection to be hosted in Hilo. This repository will not only help protect both locally available and not-yet-here coffee varieties, but those varieties will be freely available to anyone interested in having them. The global and local importance of all this scientific research in Hawai'i cannot be overstated. Research in Hawai'i has changed the way some countries prune their coffee. Work on coffee flowering has helped people all over the world better estimate water requirements for their plants throughout the year. Locally, Hawai'i's scientific community has supported or improved nearly every area of local coffee production.

ETHICAL COFFEE

Several decades ago, coffee was just coffee. It came from overseas, and most people didn't think a whole lot about its journey from the farm to their cup. Today, however, environmental and social issues rest on the minds of many people. As a result, coffee drinkers are seeking out brands that support issues such as environmental preservation, social equality and economic stability.

Several independent, third-party organizations have been established to certify farms that grow ethical coffee. The certifications reassure consumers that the growers are operating in a socially and/or environmentally responsible manner. These organizations inspect farms and, sometimes, serve as the medium of commerce for the coffee. When all is in proper order, the coffee growers earn a recognizable, certified label.

Meeting certification standards is an added expense for farmers. They typically must pay the organizations a certification fee. In addition, some environmentally friendly growing methods produce lower yields and require more labor. As an incentive for farmers to grow ethical coffee and to offset the costs, buyers offer a price premium that is sometimes set by the certifying agency. This premium is ultimately passed on to consumers in the moderately higher price of the coffee. It is an economic model that encourages consumers to pay

→ THE KONA KAI SCANDAL

In 1996, Michael Norton, owner of the California-based coffee distributor Kona Kai Farms, was caught selling coffee not grown in Kona as Kona coffee. For several years, he managed to sell millions of pounds of Costa Rican and Panamanian coffee at Kona prices and with the Kona label to reputable buyers across the US. Once the truth came out, the buyers felt foolish and the Kona farmers were divided on how to proceed. For a time, Kona's reputation took a hit.

The scandal had a big impact on Kona and the burgeoning coffee industry across the state. It led to the creation of the Hawai'i-Grown Coffee Law and it has been the backbone of conversations about blending and protecting the Kona name (and other Hawai'i origins). It is a reminder that the potential for harm to the Hawai'i coffee industry's reputation is real. The strength of the Hawai'i-origin "brand" relies on the trust of consumers.

for their philosophical and environmental beliefs. Below are descriptions of all the current ethical coffee options.

ORGANIC

Farmers and consumers who support organic agriculture believe that modern agrochemicals are dangerous to human health and to the environment. Organic growing methods differ from conventional growing techniques in that they don't use synthetically derived chemicals in the field, including pesticides such as Roundup® and manufactured fertilizers. Instead, all agrochemicals must be derived from natural products either directly (for instance, manure used for fertilizer) or as purifications of a product (such as neem oil used for pest control).

Organic certification agencies also ban the use of genetically modified (GM) crops. Currently, there are no GM coffee plants grown commercially anywhere in the world. However, several laboratories have worked on GM coffee plants. The future commercial use of any GM coffee plants will depend on both farmer and consumer sentiment.

Many farms in developing nations are organic by default: They simply cannot afford agrochemicals. However, without a third-party verification, consumers have no assurance that the coffee was, in fact, grown organically.

In Hawai'i's local coffee community, there are many strong supporters of organic agriculture. In fact, nearly all of Hawai'i's growing regions have certified organic farmers, and some local retailers ensure that organic coffee is always stocked on their shelves.

FAIR TRADE

The fair trade philosophy offers economic incentives to farmers, mostly in developing countries, for producing goods. One of the great inequalities of global trade is the price disparity between what a farmer in a developing country earns for selling green coffee and what a consumer in a developed country pays for roasted coffee.

When a coffee crisis occurs, coffee prices fall to very low levels, so low that many farmers are paid less per pound of coffee than it costs them to grow it! To address these inequalities, fair trade products, including coffee, offer a guaranteed minimum price to participating farmers. When world prices climb above the minimum, farmers are paid the difference to match it. In addition to a price minimum, fair trade regulations support a variety of social issues pertaining to farmers.

Fair trade regulations are set by the Fairtrade Labelling Organizations International (FLO) and are observed by all fair trade certifiers. Its rules are in place to protect workers and children from poor working arrangements. In addition, the regulations encourage community development in the areas of education, medicine and general well-being. The environmental regulations discourage the use of synthetic agrochemicals and encourage the protection of natural resources, as well as minimal waste production. Genetically modified organisms are not permitted under this certification.

With fair trade coffee, participating producers must be members of a cooperative or association. In effect, these groups are the actual fair trade members. The cooperative must be transparent in all of its operations, keep detailed records and be fully democratic. In addition to setting minimum coffee prices for farmers, fair trade also offers a price premium to reward farmers for endorsing socially and environmentally responsible programs. The organization offers an additional premium to organic farmers.

Because fair trade certification is designed to address inequalities for farmers in developing countries, farms in developed countries have not traditionally been included in the certification scheme, though some nut and fruit farms were certified fair trade in the United States in 2007. Based on the experience of this author, Hawai'i coffee farms adhere to the principles of fair trade philosophy.

In 2012, Fair Trade USA, the US member of the FLO, broke away from the parent organization as it felt too many farmers were being passed over by the FLO rules. Fair Trade USA not only certifies individual coffee farmers, but they also have begun certifying farms in the United States, as they believe their standards are tougher than current US labor laws. Fair Trade USA has its own certifying regulations and a unique logo (depicted). Currently, one coffee farm in Hawai'i is certified.

UTZ—RAINFOREST ALLIANCE

UTZ is a multi-commodity coffee-certifying organization that traditionally has focused on social issues at the farm level. UTZ empowers farmers to improve product quality and, consequently, attain better prices. It actively helps farmers, firstly, to operate their farms as businesses by investing in future growth and, secondly, to develop and segment the quality of products by training and mentoring growers on issues ranging from soil health and erosion prevention to coffee handling and storage techniques. On the market, UTZ links producers and buyers to create a transparent system for price negotiation. Rather than setting a minimum price like fair trade, the UTZ

WHY IS HAWAIIAN COFFEE SO EXPENSIVE?

There's no way around it, coffee grown in Hawai'i is expensive relative to most other coffees in the world. By the end of 2018, the lowest-priced green Hawaiian coffee cost about 7.5 times more than the international commodity price for coffee. There's no exact reason why it costs more, rather, several factors contribute to it.

❋ **High cost of production.** Hawai'i's distance from everything makes shipment of goods (equipment, agrochemicals, building materials, packaging, etc.) pricey. In addition, labor costs are higher than almost anywhere else in the world that grows coffee.

❋ **Rare and extraordinary land.** Hawai'i is wonderous and beautiful and there isn't much of it. Lots of people want to live and work here, not just coffee farmers. Consequently, prices for land are very, very high.

❋ **It is part of the United States of America.** This is a good thing for many reasons. However, it does mean that federal and state environmental, safety and business laws apply. While this makes coffee farming wholesome, it adds costs that other coffee origins lack.

❋ **Cost of living.** The American cost and standard of living—as well as job market competition—require higher wages paid to workers and an adequate profit margin to support the business owners, as compared to many other parts of the coffee-growing world. Hawai'i's cost of living is significantly higher than the rest of the US.

If one considers the social, economic and environmental justices that exist on a Hawai'i coffee farm, the price of the coffee isn't expensive at all. Rather, it makes the rest of world's coffee uncomfortably cheap.

system connects buyers who are willing to pay above-market prices with farmers who produce high-quality, ethically-grown coffee.

The Rainforest Alliance is a certifying agency with regulations aimed at supporting the three traditional pillars of sustainability: environmental, social and economic. This makes their regulations the most diverse among certifiers. Aspects of their regulations include biodiversity and natural resource conservation, improved livelihoods and human well-being and effective business planning and management.

In 2018, UTZ and the Rainforest Alliance merged and began the task of developing a new certification standard. The new program will integrate new technologies with proven, effective systems. In addition to a new standard, it will include a new chain of custody, a new fee structure, and a new labeling policy for companies sourcing certified products. The standard is under development and will be released and implemented in 2020.

SHADE-GROWN/ BIRD FRIENDLY COFFEE

Coffee evolved in the shaded understory of tropical forests. Biologically, the plant is well equipped to live in such a dark environment. However, under these conditions, it produces only small amounts of fruit.

From an agricultural perspective, therefore, less light means lower yield. To increase production (as most

MONKEYPOD TREES PROVIDE SHADE FOR COFFEE AT ISLAND SUN COFFEE, KONA, HAWAI'I ISLAND

farmers want to do), one must simply increase the light by growing the coffee in partial to full sun. The increase in seed production necessitates a great deal more water and nutrition than are needed by low-light plants. Without these added inputs, the coffee plant will sacrifice itself in order to support the seeds. It wasn't until the fairly recent invention of synthetic fertilizers that high production levels could be achieved in a full-sun system. Concurrently, the development of other agrochemicals (pesticides and herbicides) contributed to the success of these intensive agricultural systems. Farms across the planet began growing coffee in full sun. To do this, many areas were denuded of the existing forests to make room for the coffee.

The destruction of rainforests has caused some people to rethink the wisdom and benefits of full-sun production. In the United States, ornithologists began realizing that many North American migratory birds used the tropical forests to overwinter. As the birds' population decreased, people started an effort to find a balance between bean and bird. The Smithsonian's Migratory Bird Center began promoting coffee that was grown in shaded systems. They soon began certifying the shaded farms that were also certified organic by a USDA-certified agency.

The use of shade trees is about more than habitats and agrochemicals. Shade trees can influence the watershed, the microclimate and local soil nutrition. Furthermore, they can benefit farmers by supplying additional tree products such as mulch from leaves, food products and firewood. This has caused several other organizations to establish their own criteria and certifications for shade-grown coffee systems. Unfortunately, no single set of criteria exists for shade coffee, as is the case

MULCH NURSING AND SUPPORTING YOUNG COFFEE TREES

JULI BURDEN

STUDENT OF COFFEE

MANY PEOPLE say they'd love to study coffee in school; few people do it. Juli Burden, a coffee fiend, moved to Hawai'i to do this very thing. Juli is currently working towards a bachelor's degree in environmental soil science so that she can have an even greater impact on the coffee industry than she's already had.

Juli discovered coffee through social activism while working at her first coffee job for a Fair Trade Certified roaster in Florida. Helping farmers through fair trade was a cause she could get behind and it gave her, a budding professional photographer, exposure to specialty coffee. Yet it wasn't until a photography trip to the Philippines that she realized she wanted to work in coffee. Stumbling upon a coffee orchard, she realized that coffee and conservation could work in tandem rather than compete for space. She knew then that she wanted to dedicate her life to coffee, agricultural science and conservation.

It was clear being an art major wouldn't help her reach her goal. She looked for a science major in a place that would facilitate learning about coffee and provide a chance for a hands-on experience. Hawai'i was a natural fit. Since starting on this pathway, she's learned chemistry, biology, agriculture and a slew of other things. Most importantly, she's learned to never forget to ask "why" and, of course, to record all her observations and data.

In the course of her coffee career, she's held multiple jobs in the industry: bagger and deliverer, barista, cupper, teacher and consultant. She's even dabbled in roasting and sales. Her formal education has been supplemented with work at the Hawai'i Agriculture Research Center, where she's had real life, hands-on experience with farm management and coffee growing and processing.

Juli's passion for coffee is self-evident. She has coffee apparel, a coffee tattoo and she always works as a barista somewhere. She is a certified Q grader, she serves on the board of the Hawai'i Coffee Association and has organized and co-organized several coffee competitions in Hawai'i.

Juli's ultimate dream is to set up and host demonstration coffee agroforestry farms in biodiversity hotspots around the world, using native trees and high-value specialty crops like coffee and cacao. Using those farms, she'd teach farmers about sustainability and quality, empowering them to better succeed as coffee producers and caretakers of the earth.

for fair trade and UTZ coffees. There are two main reasons for this: First, defining what constitutes appropriate shade is very challenging because of differences in local ecologies and plant species. Also, there is no consensus on how much shade, and from what source, is best. Second, all the shade-coffee certifications actually attempt to establish criteria for a sustainable production system, not just a shaded one. These criteria include soil and water conservation, protection of biological diversity and sensitive ecological areas, safe and healthy working conditions and positive contributions to the local community. Since there is no overarching definition of sustainable coffee, no single scheme for shade-grown coffee has been proven better than any other.

In Hawai'i, very little coffee is, or ever has been, deliberately grown under tree shade. In Kona, where most of the coffee farms exist, the afternoons tend to be overcast with cloud cover. In the days before chemical fertilizers, this minimized coffee dieback and allowed farmers to produce more coffee. Both in the past and today, many farms have shade trees along field borders, near homes or even scattered throughout the fields. The trees provide wind protection, a secondary crop of other kinds of fruits and nuts or just aesthetics. Currently, there are several regions across the state where farmers plant beneath native forests or actively cultivate shade trees on their fields. Although no Hawai'i farm is certified as shade grown, research on these coffee systems has become an active part of scientific experiments in recent decades.

DIRECT TRADE

Direct trade is the newest addition to the ethical coffee group. Unlike all the others, though, it has no certification, no umbrella organization and no special label. This new model attempts to eliminate all the unknowns in the coffee-purchasing chain by connecting the roaster directly to the farmer.

Direct trade was coined and trademarked by Intelligentsia Coffee in Chicago, Illinois. The company was unsatisfied with the other ethical coffee models, yet wanted to convey that its coffees were purchased with great care and responsibility. In the search for high-quality, boutique coffees, Intelligentsia realized

> "The voodoo priest and all his powders were as nothing compared to espresso, cappuccino, and mocha, which are stronger than all the religions of the world combined, and perhaps stronger than the human soul itself."
>
> —Mark Helprin,
> *Memoir from Antproof Case*

VIRGINIA EASTON SMITH AND GARY STRAWN LEAD A WORKSHOP FOR KONA COFFEE FARMERS.

that once it discovered the right coffee, it could purchase coffee directly from the farmer or co-op and pay a fair price commensurate with the quality. Moreover, by visiting each farm annually, Intelligentsia maintains a relationship with the farmer and thus evaluates how the coffee is grown. This allows the company to select farms that are operated according to social and environmental principles that meet its approval.

While direct trade is not very common, other quality-driven roasters have begun taking this approach. They're interested in paying more for high-quality green coffee that comes from a source they are connected to and trust. This model calls for a great deal of traveling and expense, which smaller roasters may find financially prohibitive. This model also requires trust on behalf of the customer. After all, with no third-party monitoring of the farm's actions, there is no guarantee that the coffee is sourced exactly as the roaster claims.

Again, like fair trade and UTZ, Hawai'i is not necessarily an appropriate locale for the direct trade concept. The kinds of inequality found elsewhere in the world don't exist in Hawai'i. Furthermore, unlike in most other locations, consumers can engage directly with Hawai'i farmers via the internet or through actual farm visits. In addition, any purchase of green coffee by a roaster typically is made directly from the farmer, ensuring a very direct relationship.

DETAIL FROM MURAL PAINTED FOR
DAYLIGHT MIND COFFEE CO.'S KONA RESTAURANT
BY STEPHANIE BOLTON

CHAPTER 7

BEYOND THE CUP

ALTERNATIVE PRODUCTS, COFFEE CULTURE & MORE

WHILE THE TASTING of coffee is the experience we most commonly think of, the cultural and social aspects are just as important. After all, we don't drink coffee in a bubble. In Hawai'i, there are many ways to explore coffee culture. They range from a 10-day festival in Kona to farm visits on Kaua'i to coffee schools throughout the state. An enlightening, firsthand coffee experience is only a short trip away.

NOT QUITE COFFEE

Roasting and brewing coffee beans will always be the most common way of interacting with the coffee plant, but some companies in Hawai'i have recognized that there are other useful parts of the plant and that even the roasted coffee and brew can be destined for more than warming a mug.

The fruit that surrounds the coffee seed is edible. While it isn't the tastiest of fruits, when it is dried down, it can be brewed as a tea. Locally, a handful of companies offer it to consumers, often under the traditional name for it, cascara. Some companies sell it in its pure form, as just coffee fruit, while others blend it with other plants to create flavorful, complex tisanes.

Other companies make use of the coffee cherries but not for direct brewing. Rather, they use extracts of the antioxidant rich cherries to add to their beverages or roasted coffee products, thus capturing the superfood potential of coffee.

One of the oldest methods of coffee consumption is making a resurgence, of sorts. Coffee leaves, which do contain caffeine, are brewed as tea. A few global companies have begun packaging coffee leaves as a product. In Hawai'i, one beverage company featured coffee leaf extract in a line of canned teas.

With the help of bees and coffee flower nectar, at least one farm produces coffee flower honey. While they can't guarantee all the honey is made from coffee nectar, most of it probably is. The honey doesn't taste like coffee, but it does taste different from other honeys.

Another rare use of coffee flowers is to harvest them after pollination has occurred, dry them down and use them to brew a tea or make syrup. It doesn't happen often as it is a lot of work, but the taste can be well worth the effort.

Roasted coffee has long been a common additive to chocolate bars. However, why not invert the paradigm and reinvent the "chocolate" bar? One company recently released a coffee bar, made similarly to a chocolate bar, but with coffee instead of chocolate.

With the explosion of beer breweries in Hawai'i, it is only natural that companies would partner with nearby farms to produce coffee-flavored beers.

Coffee clothing is common around the state. While some clothing is actually made with coffee to create color, it is more common to find coffee-themed clothing, particularly from some of Hawai'i's most respected aloha shirt designers.

COFFEE AS MUSE

Thanks to the explosion of specialty coffee, when people think about coffee art, they often think of latte art. And why shouldn't they? The spectacular designs that can be made simply by pouring well-textured milk into espresso are artistic indeed! But milk in coffee is just one small way of making coffee art.

Coffee inspires people, it often even defines them. Thus, they want to imbue their lives with it beyond the cup, often in ways that are

DAYLIGHT MIND COFFEE COMPANY'S KONA, HAWAI'I ISLAND, LOCATION FEATURES A LARGE-SCALE MURAL BY ARTIST STEPHANIE BOLTON DEPICTING

beautiful and artful. Coffee-themed jewelry and tattoos are now commonplace. Sculptures and paintings with coffee as the subject are easily obtainable and even found in public spaces around the world. Several artists even use coffee itself as the ink for their drawings and paintings.

In a place like Hawai'i where coffee has been embedded in the psyche of the community for nearly two centuries, art and coffee often go hand in hand. Coffee art is most commonly found in Kona, where coffee affects most lives one way or another. This is most readily seen in people's homes, where paintings and coffee-themed objects often adorn walls. However, many artists have a collection of paintings where the coffee plant is the subject, though other coffee subjects can be found, too. One artist uses brewed coffee as the stain for making decorated gourds.

Coffee art is prominent at the Kona Coffee Cultural Festival in two ways. One, the festival makes wearable pins each year (see page 120) that serve as entry passes to festival events. Every year, a different artist's work is used as the image for the pin and all festival materials for that year. Second, most years, the festival hosts a contest for the best coffee-themed art piece.

Exploring Hawai'i coffee art is fairly easy. Many galleries in Kona and local artists across the state have impressive collections to share. Of course, a simple internet search will turn up plenty of images as well.

EVENTS

KONA COFFEE CULTURAL FESTIVAL

www.konacoffeefest.com

Every year since 1970, the community of Kona has hosted the Kona Coffee Cultural Festival. Held in early November, mid-harvest, the 10-day event celebrates the mighty bean that defines Kona.

The festival kicks off with The International Lantern Parade followed by a traditional bon dance. Local entertainment, food and, of course, Kona coffee samplings are available.

VARIOUS STEPS ALONG COFFEE'S JOURNEY FROM ITS EARLY ORIGINS TO MODERN ROASTING AND BREWING.

The quaint historic village of Hōlualoa hosts The Kona Coffee & Art Stroll. Each gallery partners with a farm, bringing two worlds together for an unusual partnership. As partygoers meander through town, they can easily find coffee samples and coffee-inspired apparel and art.

Ueshima Coffee Company hosts a cherry-picking experience, the Kona Historical Society offers guided tours of the Kona Coffee Living History Farm, the Donkey Mill Art Center hosts a coffee-themed art exhibit and KTA Super Stores hosts the Kona Coffee Recipe Contest.

In recent years, cafés have been hosting a latte art throwdown. Baristas from various Kona cafés gather in a fun, lighthearted environment to compete for the best latte artist in town.

The signature event of the festival is the Kona Coffee Cupping Competition. More than 60 farms submit their coffees for the two-day event. The first day, a panel of judges eliminates most of the coffees. The following day, the coffees are re-cupped to select the winners. The first-place farm claims glory, respect and bragging rights for the year.

The Kona Coffee Cultural Festival is a wonderful, high-energy event. While both locals and visitors enjoy the variety of events, locals also get the chance to step back and glow with pride over their regional treasure.

SEED TO CUP FESTIVAL

www.mauicoffeeassociation.
blogspot.com/p/seed-to-cup

The Maui Coffee Association hosts this one-day event each year to celebrate their cherished bean. The event allows visitors to meet farmers, roasters and other industry members. Numerous competitions are held throughout the day, including ones for latte art, roasting and a fashion show for clothing made from coffee paraphernalia. Of course, coffee-inspired food, coffee and entertainment are available during the entire festival.

PINS FROM THE KONA COFFEE CULTURAL FESTIVAL

KAUAI CHOCOLATE AND COFFEE FESTIVAL

www.kauaichocolateandcoffeefestival.com

Why stop with a chocolate festival when you can celebrate coffee, too? This charming two-day festival occurs annually in Hanapēpē. The coffee community joins together to offer seminars, demos and tastings of Kauaʻi's delicious brew. In addition, many local businesses set up booths to create a festive social and shopping experience.

COMPETITIONS

A hallmark of an advanced, mature coffee industry is the presence of competitions that celebrate coffee production and the skills of industry workers. Hawaiʻi has both!

The annual Kona Coffee Cultural Festival and the Hawaiʻi Coffee Association have long hosted cupping competitions to discover the extraordinary coffees grown in Hawaiʻi. Within the past decade, both organizations have followed competition systems that are used and recognized throughout the international specialty coffee community. The festival has even experimented with a novel, locally developed competition system.

Barista competitions seem to now be regular events in Hawaiʻi. In the last couple of years, Hawaiʻi has also hosted an Aeropress Competition and a US Brewers Cup competition. Both are preliminary rounds that send a winner to the national competitions.

AGTOURISM

For tourists from the US mainland, Hawaiʻi is a fantastic coffee origin to investigate. The locals speak English, they use the US dollar and the culture is just unfamiliar enough to be interesting, yet not enough to be uncomfortable. In addition, the roads are nice, the street signs are manageable and the food won't upset your stomach. In terms of ease and depth of experience, if a person wanted to see what a coffee origin is all about, Hawaiʻi is one of the best places to explore!

Hawaiʻi's agtourism has developed into a sophisticated and intricate part of the economy. Coffee farmers are interested in more than simply selling their coffee to anonymous customers. They are proud of their work and are eager to offer tours, educate, share and, oftentimes, caffeinate anyone willing to spend time on the farm.

For the consumer, agtourism offers the chance to learn the intricate process that coffee traverses from its planting as a seedling to a brew in a cup. More important, perhaps, is the opportunity to connect to a farmer and establish a direct, personal relationship. What could be better than knowing the trees your morning coffee came from and getting to meet the person whose labor got that coffee to your cup? A handful of farmers have gone beyond just opening up their farms

for visitors and tours. These farms host rental units for visitors to stay during their vacations. Generally, these farmers encourage visitors to spend time on the farm, getting a feel for the farming process.

Visiting coffee farms is an opportunity available to both visitors to the state of Hawai'i and residents. Few crops are as interesting as coffee, and few have such a rich local history. Every coffee drinker should explore the depths of this most cherished beverage. Check out the websites of farms that interest you to see what options are available.

KONA COFFEE LIVING HISTORY FARM

www.konahistorical.org

Across the state, an inquisitive person can observe and even participate in life on a modern coffee farm. However, it's more difficult to

TOP: MALIA BOLTON LEADS A FARM TOUR AT KONA COFFEE & TEA, HAWAI'I ISLAND. ABOVE: THE KONA COFFEE LIVING HISTORY FARM OFFERS REENACTMENTS OF FARM LIFE IN THE EARLY 1900S.

imagine the changes between today's farms and those of yesteryear. The Kona Coffee Living History Farm recreates a time when working the land was a different, yet in some ways similar, experience.

The Living History Farm replicates the daily life of a typical Japanese coffee farm of the period 1925–1945. The farm boasts authentic buildings, equipment and artifacts of a bygone era, while costumed interpreters replicate household and agricultural duties. The farm offers a self-guided experience where visitors encounter "farmers" and "farm wives" who can elaborate on any of the farm's areas and activities of interest.

EDUCATION

If you're reading this, then you understand coffee is more than just a cup of caffeine and you are keen to learn more about it. Books are great but sometimes, and for some people, learning requires doing or engaging with another person. In Hawai'i, several companies offer learning opportunities either at their location or one of your choosing.

COFFEA CONSULTING

www.coffeaconsulting.com

Coffea Consulting brings coffee knowledge anywhere a person wants, from a home or office to a hotel room. Seminars, private tastings and cuppings are the most common educational formats provided, however, custom classes and events are also available.

Publisher's Note: Coffea Consulting is owned and operated by the author of this book, Dr. Shawn Steiman.

DAYLIGHT MIND COFFEE COMPANY

www.daylightmind.com

Nestled on the ocean's edge, Daylight Mind has a classroom setting unmatched anywhere in the world. Daylight Mind offers lectures, hands-on brewing classes, cuppings and roasting lessons. Customized classes and events are also available.

Publisher's Note: The author, Dr. Shawn Steiman, is a partner in Daylight Mind Coffee Company.

THE AUTHOR (LEFT) EVALUATES A COFFEE'S ROAST LEVEL BEFORE BEGINNING A CUPPING SESSION

KONA COFFEE PURVEYORS

www.konacoffeepurveyors.com

Kona Coffee Purveyors hosts a certified Specialty Coffee Association lab. They offer SCA coffee skills classes and Q grader exams.

PACIFIC COFFEE RESEARCH

www.pacificcoffeeresearch.com

Pacific Coffee Research hosts a certified Specialty Coffee Association lab. They offer SCA coffee skills classes throughout the year. They also offer barista, roasting and tasting training. Custom trainings are also available.

WORLD WIDE OPPORTUNITIES ON ORGANIC FARMS

www.wwoofusa.org

There is perhaps no better way to understand coffee than to become a coffee farmer. The World Wide Opportunities on Organic Farms (WWOOF) organization provides the opportunity to work on and learn about organic farms all over the world. In Hawai'i, 354 farms currently participate in this program, 58 of which grow coffee.

....

"If you want to improve your understanding, drink coffee."

—Sydney Smith,
18th–19th century Anglican
cleric and author

....

Participating farms host volunteers by supplying food and lodging. In exchange, volunteers work the farm for one week to several months.

HAWAI'I ORGANIZATIONS

Hawai'i's small coffee community lends itself to open discussions, disagreements, similar causes, partnerships and ideas. As a result, people specializing in all aspects of coffee have formed groups to unite small coffee communities and harmonize the Hawai'i industry at large.

HAWAI'I COFFEE ASSOCIATION

www.hawaiicoffeeassoc.org

The Hawai'i Coffee Association (HCA) was formed in 1995. Its membership joins people together in every coffee sector from all islands: growers, processors, roasters and retailers. Service companies outside of the coffee industry such as agricultural product vendors, bag makers and shippers also hold membership. The HCA brings the industry sectors together to discuss labeling rules, agricultural issues, quality improvement and marketing.

The HCA hosts an annual conference in the Islands. It boasts a trade show, barista training, business meetings, guest speakers, a farm tour and industry updates. The conference is open to everyone interested in the Hawai'i coffee industry.

HAWAI'I COFFEE GROWERS ASSOCIATION

Formed in late 1989 as an outgrowth of participants in a statewide coffee variety experiment, the Hawai'i Coffee Growers Association (HCGA) concentrates on farming-related issues. While the membership consists of fairly few farms, they represent over 80 percent of the coffee acreage in the state. The group focuses on the growing and production of coffee, with most of their current energies concentrated on the HARC breeding program and pesticide registration.

KONA COFFEE COUNCIL

www.kona-coffee-council.com

The Kona Coffee Council (KCC), formed in 1985, brings together the entire coffee industry in the Kona region. Its members can be farmers, processors, roasters and retailers. With regular workshops, the KCC educates its members and consumers about all aspects of coffee. Its enduring goal is to promote and protect high-quality Kona coffee locally and internationally. The group is also a member of the HCA.

KONA COFFEE FARMERS ASSOCIATION

www.konacoffeefarmers.org

The Kona Coffee Farmers Association (KCFA) formed in 2006. The organization is also a member of the HCA. The KCFA is composed of farmers who promote and protect high-quality Kona coffee locally and internationally. In addition, they promote legislation mandating a minimum of 75 percent Kona coffee in any blend that carries the Kona name. Plus, the association rejects importation of green beans into Hawai'i, field testing and planting of GM coffee and the use of varieties other than 'Kona Typica'. The group is also a member of the HCA.

MAUI COFFEE ASSOCIATION

www.mauicoffeeassociation.com

Started in 2005, the Maui Coffee Association (MCA) unites Maui's coffee community. The MCA is a member of the HCA. The group educates people about Maui coffee, encourages and improves coffee growing, and represents the Maui coffee industry in local and state politics. It holds open, monthly meetings and sponsors education workshops for all who are interested. They also host the annual Seed to Cup festival.

COFFEE CHERRIES AFTER SOAKING IN YEAST SOLUTION

HAWAI'I BASED CONSULTANTS

For a state with so much coffee action, it isn't surprising that a handful of coffee-centric consultants call Hawai'i their home base. If you have a need for coffee assistance, there's a company here that can help you.

COFFEA CONSULTING

www.coffeaconsulting.com

This firm, led by this book's author, Dr. Shawn Steiman, works internationally throughout the coffee industry to enhance coffee knowledge and quality. Their expertise includes production, processing, roasting, sourcing, quality assessment, education, writing and event services.

COFFEE STRATEGIES

www.coffeestrategies.com

Coffee Strategies is a coffee development firm that provides value chain consulting services for government and private industry. It is led by Andrew Hetzel, an 18-year industry veteran. He has served on the Specialty Coffee Association board and was the chairman of the SCA Education Advisory Council.

DAN KUHN COFFEE CONSULTING

www.dankuhncoffee.com

This firm specializes in coffee agronomy, irrigation, mechanization, processing and marketing.

KAUAI ROASTERY LLC

www.kauairoastery.com

Kauai Roastery's core competencies include coffee farm development (production, processing and marketing) as well as being the Hawai'i agent for Netafim USA (drip irrigation systems) and Pinhalense processing equipment.

DR. ROBERT V. OSGOOD

rvosgood@aol.com

Dr. Osgood specializes in improving practices that increase yield while utilizing responsible production and processing practices.

ORGANIZATIONS BEYOND HAWAI'I

While Hawai'i is the most geographically isolated landmass in the world, its coffee industry is not isolated. Below is a list of some prominent organizations outside of the Islands in which many Hawai'i coffee people participate.

WORLD COFFEE RESEARCH

www.worldcoffeeresearch.org

World Coffee Research's mission is to grow, protect and enhance supplies of quality coffee while improving the livelihoods of the families who produce it. It accomplishes this by coordinating scientific research within or across existing research institutions. It then serves as a platform for disseminating that information.

SPECIALTY COFFEE ASSOCIATION

www.sca.coffee

By 1982 enough people had been thinking about specialty coffee to prompt the formation of the world's largest coffee trade organization—the Specialty Coffee Association of America. In 2016, it merged with its European counterpart to form the Specialty Coffee Association. The group has taken the lead in defining specialty coffee, establishing standards, training cuppers and educating the world about coffee. The SCA is an excellent resource for anyone curious about specialty coffee.

COFFEE ROASTERS GUILD

www.crg.coffee

This is a trade guild of the SCA. The members are passionate roasters who feel quality is the defining criterion for success as a roaster. The guild exists to support the development and promotion of the roasting profession. They offer and participate in a variety of educational opportunities ranging from classes to retreats.

THE BARISTA GUILD

www.baristaguild.coffee

This is a trade guild of the SCA. The guild primarily serves as a medium for discussion and education about all things related to coffee brewing. They offer and participate in a variety of educational and competitive opportunities.

COFFEE TECHNICIANS GUILD

www.coffeetechniciansguild.org

This is a trade guild of the SCA. The recently formed guild supports specialty coffee through the development of professional technicians. They aspire to provide mutual support and knowledge as well as opportunities to develop skills and learn best practices.

CUP OF EXCELLENCE

www.cupofexcellence.org

The Cup of Excellence (COE) program finds exceptional coffees in each participating country. Within a country, coffees are submitted to a series of cupping competitions that begin on a regional level and culminate in a competition judged by internationally acclaimed cuppers. The winning coffees are labeled with the prestigious Cup of Excellence Award and are sold to the highest bidder in an international auction.

FRESHLY ROASTED COFFEE IN THE COOLING TRAY OF A ROASTER

HAWAI'I'S CAFÉ SCENE

> "A coffeehouse is a place where people want to be alone, but need company to do it."
>
> —Alfred Polgar,
> Austrian essayist

There have long been fun, independent cafés in Hawai'i alongside familiar national chains. However, it was in 2011, with the opening of Beach Bum Café that the café scene began to diversify and explode. Beach Bum Café was the first of Hawai'i's modern, geeky, specialty coffeehouses. It served only Hawai'i-grown coffee, it offered no flavored syrups and it had no batch-brewed coffee (i.e., no pots of coffee). Rather, it offered only bespoke brews from the finest Hawai'i coffee farms. While Beach Bum Café didn't survive, it did prove there was interest in pushing the limits of what a cup of coffee could taste like.

Since then, geeky, specialty cafés have arisen on every major Hawaiian island. These cafés source beans from local roasters and/or famous mainland ones. The brews they offer tend to be complex and, at times, even esoteric. Typically, these coffees are brewed bespoke for each customer, though some cafés brew them in bulk.

New independent cafés, coffee carts and coffee trucks appear regularly across the Islands alongside an increasing number of national chains. Never before has Hawai'i seen such a diverse and eclectic offering of coffee options. There's a café, somewhere nearby, that offers each customer something they want.

INTERNATIONAL COFFEE ORGANIZATION

www.ico.org

Established in 1963, the International Coffee Organization (ICO) is the main intergovernmental group for coffee. It brings together producing and consuming countries to address global issues.

NATIONAL COFFEE ASSOCIATION OF U.S.A., INC.

www.ncausa.org

The National Coffee Association of U.S.A. (NCA), founded in 1911, is also a coffee trade organization. It is known for its quarterly compilation of industry statistics and annual survey of national drinking trends.

ASSOCIATION FOR SCIENCE AND INFORMATION ON COFFEE

www.asic-cafe.org

The Association for Science and Information on Coffee (ASIC) began in 1966 as a non-governmental body to study coffee science. Today, it is the only unaffiliated scientific body whose sole purpose is to facilitate communication between scientists working on all aspects of coffee. ASIC's biennial scientific conferences alternate locations between producing countries and consuming countries.

GLOBAL COMPETITIONS

Below is a list of the major global coffee competitions. They celebrate the skills of baristas, roasters and tasters, creating space and purpose to expand beyond the limits of the various disciplines. Like in all international competitions, those who compete are fueled by a passion that pushes them to train and explore their craft in ways they never expected. Each has a US counterpart which feeds into the international competition.

WORLD AEROPRESS CHAMPIONSHIP
www.worldaeropresschampionship.com

WORLD BARISTA CHAMPIONSHIP
www.worldbaristachampionship.org

WORLD BREWERS CUP CHAMPIONSHIP
www.worldbrewerscup.org

WORLD CEZVE/IBRIK CHAMPIONSHIP
www.ibrikchampionship.org

WORLD COFFEE IN GOOD SPIRITS CHAMPIONSHIP
www.worldcoffeeevents.org

WORLD COFFEE ROASTING CHAMPIONSHIP
www.worldcoffeeroasting.org

WORLD CUP TASTERS CHAMPIONSHIP
www.worldcuptasters.org

WORLD LATTE ART CHAMPIONSHIP
www.worldlatteart.org

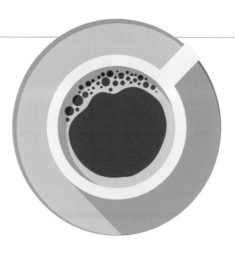

AFTERWORD

FOR SOME 200 YEARS, coffee has been a part of the Hawai'i landscape. It has percolated through many lives and has influenced many others. In its early years, it survived a major pest infestation, the many ups and downs of the global coffee market, a major scandal in the 1990s and the introduction of the coffee berry borer. As of 2014, there were more coffee farms in Hawai'i than there have been since the early 1960s. In addition, the café scene is stronger and more diverse than ever.

The Hawai'i coffee industry is not only healthy and strong, it is blossoming. It will continue to be a significant part of the Hawai'i economy and culture for a long, long time. Nonetheless, it will face several significant challenges in the coming years that will require ingenuity and endurance to overcome.

The most immediate challenge is the dwindling supply of pickers to harvest the coffee. Intense field labor, like picking coffee, is less and less appealing to many people each year. Hawai'i farmers have been feeling this strain for several years already. It is only going to get worse. The likely solution will involve innovative technology. While large-scale mechanical harvesters are used on some local farms, their design, size and cost prevent their widespread use throughout the state. University of Hawai'i researchers began exploring small mechanical harvesting devices in the 1960s and have dabbled with them ever since. Researchers elsewhere have tinkered with the technology, too. It is a tricky problem to solve, but one that will need solutions soon.

As with farming everywhere, the average age of coffee farmers seems to be creeping up. Few young people are interested in the rigors of farming coffee coupled with the challenges of marketing and selling it, too. While this seems like it should be a problem for Hawai'i coffee, it apparently is not; the number of coffee farms in Hawai'i has been increasing. Most of these new farmers are probably retirees or people in a position to start a new career as a farmer. So long as the lifestyle and romance continues to appeal to people, there will be ample interest in coffee farming in Hawai'i.

The high prices commanded by Hawai'i-grown coffee are not going to recede. If anything, they will increase over time. High prices won't cripple the industry but they will likely limit its reach. The industry will need concerted effort to educate both residents and non-residents the true value of Hawai'i-grown coffee with the hope that consumers will be willing to embrace those values with their purchasing decisions.

There are two major coffee diseases, both fungi, that have not yet reached Hawai'i: coffee berry disease (*Colletotrichum kahawae*) and coffee leaf rust, also known as roya (*Hemileia vastatrix*). Coffee berry disease has not yet left the African continent, so it is unlikely to reach Hawai'i any time soon. Coffee leaf rust, however, is in nearly every coffee growing region on the planet. Hawai'i is one of the rare exceptions. Unfortunately, it is only a matter of time before coffee leaf rust arrives and wreaks havoc on the coffee fields. Strategies exist for dealing with the fungus, though, of course, they will take time to understand and implement and they'll have undesirable time and resource costs. It might be ugly for a few years, but the industry survived the coffee berry borer and will likely survive the leaf rust.

As the specialty coffee segment continues to grow, consumers will expect more and more Hawai'i farmers to produce compelling and esoteric coffees that will fulfill their desires. To engage those customers, farmers will need to diversify the coffee varieties in their fields. While some farmers have already embraced varieties besides 'Kona Typica', many more will have to explore the flavor potentials of other varieties. Moreover, careful variety selection can be an excellent tool for combating diseases, something Hawai'i farmers will need to consider when coffee leaf rust arrives.

The Hawai'i coffee industry has a rich and diverse history and culture. It will never give up that identity. Moving forward, the industry will do as it always has done: adapt to the current conditions, adopt new technologies and engage new ideas that will benefit everyone.

THE AUTHOR'S PORTRAIT APPEARS
IN THE STORY OF COFFEE MURAL
AT DAYLIGHT MIND COFFEE COMPANY

ACKNOWLEDGMENTS

AS WITH MOST THINGS, this book would not exist if it had been left to just one person. Without question, this book would be less interesting, factually accurate and beautiful without the assistance of a great many people. To all of them, I am eternally grateful.

I especially want to thank Skip Bittenbender for giving me the opportunity to write the first edition of this book and encouraging me to do so, all the while allowing me to postpone completing my dissertation. Furthermore, his careful edits, comments and teachings have been invaluable in the making of this book. Loren Gautz earns credit for editing and fact checking. I appreciate JD Baker's surfacing for long enough to offer anthropologically rich comments.

I thank Julia Wieting for writing the blissful epigraph. In addition, her comments and editorial acumen made this book far better than anything I could have done on my own. More importantly, though, I appreciate her mental and emotional support during the times when I most struggled with being a writer and not just a scientist.

The crew at Watermark Publishing has been fantastic during the entire process. Not only did they give me the opportunity to write this book, but they also helped me along every step of the way. Thank you, Dawn Sakamoto and George Engebretson, for thinking round two of this book was a good idea. I thank Jeremy Lips for supplying so many mouth-watering food photos.

I thank all the people in the various groups, organizations, cafés, roasters and farms listed herein who contributed to the accuracy of the information within the book. Lastly, I thank all the people who contributed the photos I never thought to take.

RESOURCES

SCIENTIFIC INSTITUTIONS

Hawai'i Agriculture Research Center
www.harc-hspa.com

University of Hawai'i's College of Tropical Agriculture and Human Resources
www.cms.ctahr.hawaii.edu

TRADE JOURNALS AND MAGAZINES

BeanScene Magazine
www.beanscenemag.com.au

Caffeine
www.caffeinemag.com

Café Culture International
www.cafeculture.com

Coffee Magazine
www.coffeemagazine.co.za

Coffee & Cocoa International
www.coffeeandcocoa.net

Comunicaffe
www.comunicaffe.com

Crema
www.cremamagazine.com.au

Barista Magazine
www.baristamagazine.com

Drift
www.driftmag.com

Global Coffee Report
www.gcrmag.com

Roast Magazine
www.roastmagazine.com

Fresh Cup Magazine
www.freshcup.com

Coffee Talk
www.coffeetalk.com

Standart
www.standartmag.com

STiR
www.stir-tea-coffee.com

Tea and Coffee Trade Journal
www.teaandcoffee.net

BOOKS

A Cup of Aloha: The Kona Coffee Epic by Gerald Kinro, University of Hawai'i Press, 2003

All About Coffee by William Ukers, Martino Publishing, 2007

Coffee: A Comprehensive Guide to the Bean, the Beverage, and the Industry by Robert Thurston, Jonathan Morris and Shawn Steiman (eds), Rowman and Littlefield, 2013

Coffee: A Global History by Jonathan Morris, Reaktion Books Ltd., 2019

Coffee and Wine: Two Worlds Compared by Morten Scholer, Matador, 2018

Coffee: Growing, Processing, Sustainable Production: A Guidebook for Growers, Processors, Traders, and Researchers by Jean Nicolas Wintgens, Wiley-VC, 2004

The Craft and Science of Coffee by Britta Folmer (ed), Elsevier, 2017

Espresso Coffee, Second Edition: The Science of Quality by Rinantonio Viani and Andrea Illy (eds), Academic Press, second edition, 2004

God in a Cup by Michaele Weissman, Houghton Mifflin Harcourt, 2008

Growing Coffee in Hawai'i by H. Bittenbender and V. Smith, College of Tropical Agriculture and Human Resources, University of Hawai'i at Mānoa, 2004

The Kona Coffee Story: Along the Hawai'i Belt Road by Akemi Kikumura, Eiichiro Azuma, and Darcie C. Iki, Japanese American National Museum, 1995

The Little Coffee Know-It-All by Shawn Steiman, Quarry Books, 2015

Specialty Coffee: Managing Quality by Thomas Oberthür, Peter Läderach, H. A. Jürgen Pohlan and James H. Cock (eds), International Plant Nutrition Institute, Southeast Asia Program, 2012

Uncommon Grounds: The History of Coffee and How It Transformed Our World by Mark Pendergrast, Basic Books, second edition, 2010

Where the Wild Coffee Grows by Jeff Koehler, Bloomsbury, 2017

World Atlas of Coffee by James Hoffman, Firefly Books, second edition, 2018

SHOPPING

Visions Espresso
www.visionsespresso.com

Whole Latte Love
www.wholelattelove.com

Prima Coffee Equipment
www.prima-coffee.com

Espresso Parts
www.espressoparts.com

Seattle Coffee Gear
www.seattlecoffeegear.com

CAFÉS AND ROASTERS IN HAWAI'I

A regularly updated list is posted at the author's website, Coffea Consulting
www.coffeaconsulting.com

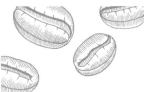

COFFEE

: _____

DATE AND TIME

Attribute

Dry Aroma

| | | | | | | | | | |
1 2 3 4 5 6 7 8 9 10

Wet Aroma

| | | | | | | | | | |
1 2 3 4 5 6 7 8 9 10

Acidity

| | | | | | | | | | |
1 2 3 4 5 6 7 8 9 10

Coffeeness

| | | | | | | | | | |
1 2 3 4 5 6 7 8 9 10

Sweetness

| | | | | | | | | | |
1 2 3 4 5 6 7 8 9 10

Body

| | | | | | | | | | |
1 2 3 4 5 6 7 8 9 10

Aftertaste

| | | | | | | | | | |
1 2 3 4 5 6 7 8 9 10

Descriptors/Defects/Comments

_____

| | | | | | | | | | |
1 2 3 4 5 6 7 8 9 10

_____

| | | | | | | | | | |
1 2 3 4 5 6 7 8 9 10

_____

| | | | | | | | | | |
1 2 3 4 5 6 7 8 9 10

_____

| | | | | | | | | | |
1 2 3 4 5 6 7 8 9 10

_____

| | | | | | | | | | |
1 2 3 4 5 6 7 8 9 10

─ *The* ─
HAWAI'I
COFFEE
Book
BY SHAWN STEIMAN

LUATION

 : _____

 : _____

COFFEE SAMPLES

7 8 9 10   1 2 3 4 5 6 7 8 9 10   1 2 3 4 5 6 7 8 9 10

7 8 9 10   1 2 3 4 5 6 7 8 9 10   1 2 3 4 5 6 7 8 9 10

7 8 9 10   1 2 3 4 5 6 7 8 9 10   1 2 3 4 5 6 7 8 9 10

7 8 9 10   1 2 3 4 5 6 7 8 9 10   1 2 3 4 5 6 7 8 9 10

7 8 9 10   1 2 3 4 5 6 7 8 9 10   1 2 3 4 5 6 7 8 9 10

7 8 9 10   1 2 3 4 5 6 7 8 9 10   1 2 3 4 5 6 7 8 9 10

7 8 9 10   1 2 3 4 5 6 7 8 9 10   1 2 3 4 5 6 7 8 9 10

7 8 9 10   1 2 3 4 5 6 7 8 9 10   1 2 3 4 5 6 7 8 9 10

7 8 9 10   1 2 3 4 5 6 7 8 9 10   1 2 3 4 5 6 7 8 9 10

7 8 9 10   1 2 3 4 5 6 7 8 9 10   1 2 3 4 5 6 7 8 9 10

7 8 9 10   1 2 3 4 5 6 7 8 9 10   1 2 3 4 5 6 7 8 9 10

Scale: not present ▬▬▬▬▬▬ intense

GLOSSARY

ACIDITY This organoleptic characteristic is best described by the bright, lively, tingly sensation associated with citrus fruits and vinegar.

AFTERTASTE This organoleptic characteristic refers to the intensity of the coffeeness perceived in the mouth after the coffee has been expectorated.

ARABICA The common name of the coffee species *Coffea arabica*.

AROMA This organoleptic characteristic is the intensity of the smell of coffee both when the coffee is just dry grounds and after it has been brewed. The aroma can often be used to discern a coffee's freshness, off-flavors, roast level and, occasionally, descriptors.

BARISTA A person whose profession is making coffee, typically in a coffeehouse.

BLADE GRINDER A grinder that uses a whirling metal blade to chop and bash coffee beans into smaller particles. It is the cheapest type of coffee grinder but produces non-uniform-sized particles and can easily overheat the grounds.

BLENDED COFFEE Typically it refers to a combination of coffees from different origins and/or coffees of different roast levels. However, it could also mean a combination of coffees from different farms within a region or even of different varieties or cherry processes from a single farm.

BODY This is a tactile organoleptic characteristic. It describes how viscous or thick the coffee feels on the tongue.

BURR GRINDER A grinder that uses burrs to create uniformly sized coffee grounds. It is generally more expensive than other types of grinders, but it doesn't overheat the grounds and can be easily adjusted to create different grind sizes.

COFFEENESS The paradigmatic flavor experience we think of as coffee. This word is intended to improve and supercede the word "flavor."

CUPPER A person who analyzes coffee by cupping.

CUPPING The formal method of tasting coffee that uses unfiltered coffee and spoons for slurping. The coffee is then spit out and rated on predetermined taste characteristics. Most cupping formats also include an opportunity to use novel terms to describe the brew, similar to descriptors used in wine tasting.

DIRECT TRADE A scheme of coffee trading in which the roaster has an intimate relationship with the farm it directly buys its coffee from.

DRUM ROASTER A type of coffee roaster that works by conducting heat from a flame or electric coil to a rotating metal drum that contains the coffee.

ESPRESSO This method of brewing coffee is defined as seven to nine grams of coffee packed under 30 to 40 pounds of pressure extracted with one to two ounces of ~200°F water at nine bars of pressure for 20 to 30 seconds.

ESTATE COFFEE The coffee is under the ownership of a single person from the orchard through roasting, and usually all the way to the consumer.

FAIR TRADE A certification scheme that ensures the producers of an item receive a fair price and create the product in an environmentally and socially responsible way.

FLAVOR This organoleptic characteristic is the essence of the cup. It encompasses our definition of what coffee tastes like, its coffeeness.

FLUIDIZED BED / HOT AIR ROASTER A type of coffee roaster that uses rapidly moving hot air to roast coffee.

FRUIT DRIED PROCESS A method of processing coffee cherries that forgoes removal of the skin, pulp and mucilage before drying.

FULL-IMMERSION BREWING A form of brewing coffee where the coffee and water are mixed for several minutes before filtering.

GRAVITY-FED/ PERCOLATION BREWING A form of brewing coffee where water is allowed to trickle down through a bed of coffee grounds and a filter.

GREEN COFFEE Dried, unroasted coffee that is bluish-green in color. This is the coffee of commerce.

MECHANICAL DEMUCILAGING A method of processing coffee cherries that removes the mucilage immediately after pulping using pressure and rubbing by mechanical agitation. This eliminates the need to ferment the beans before drying.

MUCILAGE This is a liquid, sticky layer that surrounds the seed and parchment and is usually removed before drying the coffee.

ONE-WAY VALVE A plastic disc inserted in coffee bags that allows coffee-derived gases to escape but prevents oxygen-rich air from entering the bag. It is used to prolong the freshness of roasted coffee.

ORGANIC A method of farming that forbids genetically modified crops and the use of synthetic agrochemicals on the farm.

ORGANOLEPTIC The term used to describe something that is experienced by the human senses.

PARCHMENT DRIED PROCESS A method of processing coffee cherries where the pulp and mucilage are removed before the seed is dried.

PARCHMENT The rough, papery layer surrounding the coffee seed. When the parchment is still attached to the dried seed, the coffee is called parchment coffee. This is the form coffee is stored in before shipping.

PEABERRY A type of coffee bean that occurs when only one seed develops in a coffee cherry. Peaberries are generally smaller than other seeds and oval shaped.

PRESSURIZED BREWING A form of brewing coffee that uses pressurized water in the brewing process.

PULP DRIED PROCESS A method of processing coffee cherries where the pulp is removed and the mucilage left on before the seed is dried.

ROAST LEVEL This is the color level to which a coffee is roasted. Many different names are used to describe the roast level; however, they are not standardized. The roast level of a coffee has a large influence on its organoleptic quality.

ROAST PROFILE The unity of the length of the roast, temperatures at various stages during the roast and the end color of the roasted bean.

ROBUSTA The common name for the coffee species *Coffea canephora.*

SHADE-GROWN / BIRD FRIENDLY A certification that ensures the coffee was grown under a certain amount and type of shade tree coverage.

SILVERSKIN This is an extremely thin layer that can adhere tightly to the coffee seed itself. It readily flakes off during roasting. At that point, it is called chaff.

SPECIALTY COFFEE Sometimes known as gourmet or premium coffee. It usually offers distinctive flavors and unique characteristics, in contrast to canned and dehydrated coffees.

SINGLE-ORIGIN COFFEE A roasted coffee product that is composed of coffee from a single country, geographical region or farm.

STRENGTH A measure of the coffee/water ratio used to brew coffee. It is not a measure of any organoleptic characteristic, though it does influence the organoleptic experience.

SWEETNESS This organoleptic characteristic is a subtle, sweet taste in the coffee that reminds us of the taste we associate with sucrose (table sugar).

VARIETY A genetically distinct population of a species that is different enough to get its own grouping but not different enough to be its own species. In coffee, varieties differ in traits such as plant stature, yield potential, bean flavor, environmental adaptation, seed size and cherry color.

BIBLIOGRAPHY

"2017 State Agriculture Overview." https://www.nass.usda.gov/Quick_Stats/Ag_Overview/stateOverview.php?state=HAWAII, accessed 9-5-18.

Alvim, P. 1985. "Coffea." CRC Handbook of Flowering, Vol II, ed. Abraham Halevy, p 308–316. CRC Press, Inc., Boca Raton, FL. pp 526.

Armstrong, L. 2002. "Caffeine, body-fluid electrolyte balance, and exercise performance." International Journal of Sport Nutrition and Exercise Metabolism. 12:189–206.

Bloxam, A. 1925. Diary of Andrew Bloxam, naturalist of the "Blonde" on her trip from England to the Hawaiian Islands, 1824-25. Honolulu: Bernice P. Bishop Museum Special Publication 10. 96 pp.

Borrell, B. 2012. "Plant biotechnology: Make it a decaf: The enduring quest for a coffee bean without the buzz." https://www.nature.com/news/plant-biotechnology-make-it-a-decaf-1.10212, accessed 8-28-18.

Carvalho, A.; Ferwerda, F.; Frahm-Leliveld, J.; Medina, D.; Mendes, A.; Monaco, L. 1969. "Coffee." Outlines of Perennial Crop Breeding in the Tropics, F. Ferwerdaand and F. Wit (eds.), pp 189–241. H. Veenman and Zonen N.V. Wageningen, The Netherlands. pp 511.

Carvalho, C. (ed). 2007. Cultivares de Café. Brasília: EMBRAPA. pp 58.

Coste, R. 1992. Coffee: The Plant and the Product. Macmillian Press, Ltd., London. pp 328.

Cramer, P. 1957. A Review of Literature of Coffee Research in Indonesia. Inter-American Institute of Agricultural Sciences, Turrialba, Costa Rica.

Crawford, D. 1937. Hawaii's Crop Parade: A review of useful products derived from the soil in the Hawaiian Islands, Past and Present. Honolulu: Advertiser Publishing Co., Ltd. pp. 305.

Davis, A., Govaerts, R., Bridson, D., and P. Stoffelen. 2006. "An annotated taxonomic conspectus of the genus Coffea (Rubiaceae)." Botanical Journal of the Linnean Society. 152:465–512.

"Food and agriculture data." Food and Agriculture Organization of the United Nations. http://www.fao.org/faostat/en/#home, accessed 8-29-2018.

Gast, R. 2002. Don Francisco de Paula Marin: A biography. Agnes C. Conrad, ed. Honolulu: University of Hawai'i Press. pp. 344.

Golovnin, V. 1979. *Around the World on the Kamchatka, 1817-1819.* Translated by Ella Wiswell. Honolulu: University of Hawai'i Press. pp. 353.

Goto, Y. B. 1982. "Ethnic groups and the coffee industry in Hawaii." *Hawaiian Journal of History.* 16:111–124.

Hawai'i State Archives, Francisco de Paula Marin Collection, M-102, Safe extracts of Marin's journal translated by Robert C. Wyllie, 1847.

Higdon, J. and B. Frei. 2006. "Coffee and health: A review of recent human research." *Critical Reviews in Food Science and Nutrition.* 46:101–123.

Kinro, Gerald. 2003. *A Cup of Aloha: The Kona Coffee Epic.* University of Hawai'i Press.

Koehler, Jeff. 2017. *Where the Wild Coffee Grows.* Bloomsbury. New York. Chapter 5.

Leliveld, J. 1940. "Onstaan en voorkomen van rondboon en vossboon bij koffie." *Bergcultures.* 14(43):1358–1362.

Monge, F. 1962. "Frecuencia de café caracolillo en plantas provenientes de semillas irradiadas." *Turrialba.* 12(4):209–210.

"organoleptic, adj." OED Online. Sept. 2004. Oxford University Press. 19 Nov. 2007 http://dictionary.oed.com/cgi/entry/00333696.

Pacific Region – Hawaii, Coffee Marketings, Final Season Estimates. https://www.nass.usda.gov/Statistics_by_State/Hawaii/Publications/Fruits_and_Nuts/201807FinalCoffee.pdf, accessed 8-29-2018.

Purseglove, J. 1968. "*Coffea arabica* L." Tropical Crops: Dicotyledons. p 458–492. Longman Group Limited, London. pp 719.

Rhodes, G. 1851. "Essay, On the Cultivation of the Coffee Treee and Manufacture of its Produce, Written for the Royal Hawaiian Agricultural Society." *Transactions of the Royal Hawaiian Agricultural Society.* 1(2):54–71.

Ricketts, T., Daily, D., Ehrlich, P. and C. Michener. 2004. "Economic value of tropical forest to coffee production." *Proceedings of the National Academy of Sciences.* 101(34):12579–12582.

Silvarolla, M., Mazzafera, P. and L. Fazuoli. 2004. "A naturally decaffeinated arabica coffee." *Nature.* 429:826.

"Statistics of Hawaii Agriculture 2011." 2013. pp. 97. https://www.nass.usda.gov/Statistics_by_State/Hawaii/Publications/Annual_Statistical_Bulletin/2011/2011HawaiiAgStats.pdf, accessed 1-25-2019.

Thompson, David. 2005. "Roots Revival." *Hana Hou.* http://www.hanahou.com/pages/magazine.asp?Action=DrawArticle&ArticleID=115&MagazineID=6, accessed 3-6-2008.

ANTIQUE COFFEE EQUIPMENT AT HAWAII COFFEE COMPANY, HONOLULU, O'AHU. FROM LEFT: A TWO-BARRELED SAMPLE ROASTER, COFFEE URN, CUPPING SPITOONS AND A GRINDER.

Top 20 commodities State of Hawaii, 2016. https://www.nass.usda.gov/Statistics_by_State/Hawaii/Publications/Miscellaneous/2016Hawaii Top20Commodities.pdf, accessed 8-29-2018.

"USDA - Hawaii Coffee Marketings, Final Season Estimates," August 19, 2015.

van der Vossen, H. 1985. "Coffee selection and breeding." *Coffee: Botany, Biochemistry and Production of Beans and Beverage*, M. Clifford and K. Willson, (eds.), p 48-96. Croom Helm, Ltd. London. pp 457.

von Faber, F. 1910. "Een en ander over de biologie van de koffiebloem." *Teysmannia* 21:556–577.

Wormer, T. 1966. Shape of bean in *Coffea arabica* L. in Kenya. *Turrialba*. 16(3):221–236.

Wyllie, R. 1850. "Wyllie's Address, Read before the Royal Hawaiian Agricultural Society, on the 12th of August, 1850". *The Transactions of the Royal Hawaiian Agricultural Society: Including a Record of the Proceedings Preliminary to the formation of the society, in August, 1850*. Honolulu: Henry M. Whitney, Government Press. 1(1):36-49.

PHOTO CREDITS

Page 42 – Shawn Steiman

Page 44 – Kauai Coffee Co.

Page 45 – MauiGrown Coffee

Page 46 – Daylight Mind Coffee Co.

Page 49 – Coffee Taster's Flavor Wheel by SCA and WCR (©2016); original image cropped to fit

Page 50 – Daylight Mind Coffee Co.

Page 51 – Daylight Mind Coffee Co.

Page 53 – Daylight Mind Coffee Co.

Page 55 – Shawn Steiman

Page 56 (blade grinder) – Tatyana Abramovich/Shutterstock.com

Page 56 (burr grinder) – Onila Farms

Page 58 – Arthur Enselme/ Shutterstock.com

Page 59 – Courtesy of Andrew Hetzel

Page 60 – Daylight Mind Coffee Co.

Page 61 (vacuum pot) – Aedka Studio/Shutterstock.com

Page 61 (espresso maker) – Hawaii Coffee Co.

Pages 66 through 96 – Jeremy Lips, styling by Christine Langfeld

Page 98 – Soni Pomaski

Page 100 – Shawn Steiman

Page 102 – Jaime Schoenhals

Page 104 – Dawn Sakamoto Paiva for Waialua Estate Coffee & Chocolate

Page 106 (top) – Shawn Steiman

Page 106 (bottom) – Shawn Steiman

Page 111 – Shawn Steiman

Page 112 – David Roche

Page 113 – Courtesy of Juli Burden

Page 115 – Valerie Strawn

Page 116 – Muralist: Stephanie Bolton; photographed by Colin Finn

Page 117-118 – Muralist: Stephanie Bolton; photographed by Dawn Sakamoto Paiva

Page 120 – Various artists for Kona Coffee Cultural Festival; photographed by Dawn Sakamoto Paiva

Page 121 – Shawn Steiman

Page 122 – Kona Coffee Living History Farm

Page 123 – Daylight Mind Coffee Co.

Page 125 – Rusty's Hawaiian

Page 127 – Mountain Thunder Coffee Plantation

Page 128 – Daylight Mind Coffee Co.

Page 132 – Muralist: Stephanie Bolton; photographed by Colin Finn

Page 143 – Hawaii Coffee Co.

Pages 146 through 149 – courtesy of the contributors

Page 160 – Yong Jaehoon

CONTRIBUTORS

ASH DANAO is a Hawai'i Island native who discovered his love of cooking from preparing family lū'aus. He trained at the West Hawai'i Culinary Arts Program and has worked at numerous restaurants on the Kona coast, including Daylight Mind Coffee Company. He currently works at the Four Seasons Resort Hualālai.

LYNDON HONDA spearheads culinary operations for Sheraton Maui Resort & Spa as the resort's executive chef. With more than 25 years in the culinary industry, he has a global approach to food, taking inspiration from an array of cultures and cuisines. Honda is a graduate of the Culinary Institute of the Pacific, Kapi'olani. Prior to taking his position at Sheraton Maui, he provided private chef services and culinary consulting through his company Laulima Events and Catering in Maui and has helped open some of Maui's most successful restaurants, including Maui Brewing Company. Honda serves on the culinary advisory board for Maui Culinary Academy.

ABIGAIL LANGLAS owns Cake Works, a full-service bakery and specialty cake shop. Chef Abi is a cake designer and culinary artist. She previously served as pastry chef for the award-winning Honolulu Coffee Company and Alan Wong's Restaurant. She is also a culinary instructor at Leeward Community College. Chef Abi was raised in Hilo, Hawai'i, but her love of pastry arts led her to Europe. In England, she received her culinary training and a diploma in advanced pastry. She then went to work in Lyon, France, creating desserts at fine-dining establishments.

QUINN MEARS loves mezcal, coffee and long walks on the beach. He's a Cancer but doesn't really know what that means. He puts his pants on one foot at a time. He's been a barkeep for several years, with a stint at Pint and Jigger in Honolulu. Following his time at Pint and Jigger, he helped open Encore Saloon and has recently joined Young's Market Company as a sales representative.

MARK NOGUCHI is a graduate of the Culinary Institute of the Pacific and the Culinary Institute of America. Noguchi's dedication to empowering his community through food and education has landed him a spot as a leader in Hawai'i's sustainable food movement. "Gooch," as his peers and friends know him, is an alum of TOWN Restaurant and Chef Mavro. He is the former co-owner and chef of He'eia Kea Pier General Store & Deli where his dedication towards sourcing product within an *ahupua'a* (traditional Hawaiian land division) garnered international attention. He then went on to form Pili Group with his wife, Amanda Corby Noguchi. Pili is a non-traditional food group focused on the connection between community, education and food. Noguchi's most recent endeavor is serving as a food catalyst at Punahou's Learning Commons.

SONI POMASKI began her professional career as a teen working at Honolulu Coffee Company where she fell in love with the process of making coffee, especially latte art. From there she spent the next 10 years working in cafés and restaurants in Honolulu and New York City. In 2013 she moved to the Big Island of Hawai'i with her husband, Mark. With his brother, Tedd, the couple opened Full Moon Café in downtown Hilo. In 2014, the restaurant, now run solely by Mark and Soni, was renamed Moon & Turtle. Along with running the daily operations of the restaurant, Soni continues to make coffee.

YEHUDA "WOODY" AND AVIVA PLAUT have been farming, gardening and cooking their whole lives. They set up the first certified organic farm (#00001) in Kentucky in 1990. As proprietors of Prosperity Farms, they ran a national gourmet condiment business using produce grown on their farm. Over their many years of playing with food, they have won recipe contests across the US, including the annual Kona Coffee Cultural Festival contest on Hawai'i Island, where they now reside.

MARTIN RATHBUN worked in numerous fields prior to training at Le Cordon Bleu, including being a printing company bindry manager and a medical examiner. In his culinary career, he has been a pastry chef at the Four Seasons Resort Hualālai. He is a co-owner of Daylight Mind Coffee Company and also owns and operates Marty Cakes & Company bakery.

GENO SARMIENTO has been with Tri-Star Restaurant Group since 1992, starting in the kitchen pantry and eventually taking the reins as corporate executive chef at Nick's Fishmarket Maui. Sarmiento has overseen the opening of Sarento's on the Beach, Son'z Steakhouse and Manoli's Pizza Company. He is a managing partner in Son'z Steakhouse. Sarmiento's appreciation of cooking came from his lola (Filipino for "grandmother").

GIDA SNYDER is chef/owner of 552 Culinary Group, LLC, a locally focused food service collaborative on the island of Kaua'i. 552 Culinary Group's companies include Gida's Kitchen In-Flight Catering and Gida's Kitchen Pantry, a line of small-batch preserved food products handcrafted with Island ingredients, launched in 2018. The company's "POG" Soda Syrup & Cocktail Mixer won a 2019 Good Food Award, recognizing sustainable, socially responsible craft producers.

SHANNON WIENER is a cook and baker with a passion for naturally fermented sourdough breads and products. Most recently he was the owner and pizza maker of Fire Dance Pizza on Oʻahu's North Shore, the first naturally fermented pizzeria in the state of Hawaiʻi.

LEE ANNE WONG lives in Maui with her fiancé and son. She enjoys steamy cups of single-origin coffee, always black, to get her day started, whether she's in the kitchen or on the road traveling for work. She appeared as a cheftestant on season one of Bravo's series *Top Chef* and has served as a supervising culinary producer for the show and its spin-off, *Top Chef Masters*. She is the chef-owner of Koko Head Café in Kaimukī, Oʻahu, and author of the cookbook *Dumplings All Day Wong*.

JEREMY LIPS is a New York City–based food, product and conceptual advertising photographer. His passion for theatrical lighting and advertising made photography a natural fit. Jeremy has shot for *Reader's Digest*, *Consumer Reports*, *Hotels at Home* and many others. He is currently the Emerging Artist chair for the New York chapter of American Photographic Artists.

INDEX OF RECIPES

INDEX

ABOUT THE AUTHOR

DR. SHAWN STEIMAN'S passion for coffee began early when he emulated his mother by drinking it in elementary school. While studying biology at Oberlin College, he focused his classwork on coffee, when possible. He even began teaching coffee classes to fellow students.

In order to grok coffee, he enrolled in the horticulture master's program at the University of Hawai'i. Deciding he liked being a coffee scientist, he continued with the PhD program in the reorganized department of Tropical Plant and Soil Sciences.

Dr. Steiman is the owner of Coffea Consulting, a coffee-centric company that works with every aspect of the coffee industry, locally, nationally and internationally. He is also a co-owner of Daylight Mind Coffee Company, a coffee roaster, coffeehouse, coffee school, restaurant and event space.

A co-editor of and contributor to *Coffee: A Comprehensive Guide to the Bean, the Beverage, and the Industry* (2013, Rowman and Littlefield), he also wrote *The Little Coffee Know-It-All: A Miscellany for Growing, Roasting, and Brewing, Uncompromising and Unapologetic* (2015, Quarto Publishing Group USA, Inc).

While Shawn is highly devoted to all things coffee, he also has a deep love of whiskey, bridge, cooking and reading. Shawn lives in Honolulu, Hawai'i, with his wife, Julia, and daughter, T'hom.